Leading from Example

A short guide to the lessons of literature

Peter Villiers

Published in this edition in 2011 by:
Triarchy Press
Station Offices
Axminster
Devon. EX13 5PF
United Kingdom

+44 (0)1297 631456
info@triarchypress.com
www.triarchypress.com

Published by Triarchy Press in 2011.

© Peter Villiers 2011

The right of Peter Villiers to be identified as the author of this book has been asserted by him in accordance with the Copyright, Designs and Patents Act, 1988.

All rights reserved.

No part of this publication may be reproduced, stored in a retrieval system or transmitted in any form or by any means including photocopying, electronic, mechanical, recording or otherwise, without the prior written permission of the publisher.

A catalogue record for this book is available from the British Library.

Cover design and image by Heather Fallows -
www.whitespacegallery.org.uk

ISBN: 978-1-908009-35-7

Contents

FOREWORD v
Jonathan Gosling

INTRODUCTION 1

CHAPTER 1 9
Where East Meets West: Rudyard Kipling

CHAPTER 2 29
The Sea Wolf: Jack London

CHAPTER 3 47
For Whom the Bell Tolls: Ernest Hemingway

CHAPTER 4 71
Leadership and bureaucracy: Joseph Conrad and *The Secret Agent*

CHAPTER 5 97
When the clock strikes thirteen: George Orwell

CHAPTER 6 117
Journey's End?: R C Sherriff

CONCLUSION 141

Bibliography 149

Index 153

In memory of my beloved Carolyn,
who died 18 December 2010

FOREWORD

Jonathan Gosling

The study of leadership requires us to imagine what it is like to be a leader, and this collection of essays shows what we can learn about leadership from works of fiction. A novelist or playwright can explore the inner workings of a character with greater veracity than the autobiographer or the historian. The measure of truth is not 'did it happen this way?', but 'do I recognize this as authentically human?' If the answer is 'yes' we acknowledge the possibility that we too might have felt, behaved or responded in these ways; and we find ourselves inside the imagined lives of these fictional characters.

The process of falling for a character, becoming irrevocably intrigued and sympathetic, is out of place in organizational life, where it must be juxtaposed with the norms of bureaucratic impersonality. But most organizations are awash with gossip and storytelling, much of it scurrilous. When people spend time talking about what is going on behind the closed doors of the management meeting, or what is motivating their leaders, or speculating about the outcomes of a current change programme, they are creating fictions, and using them to conjure a place for themselves as both authors and characters in what is essentially a constantly woven narrative.

So when we read compelling works of fiction, we are immersing ourselves in processes not so different to those of normal organizational life. The predicaments are perhaps more economically selected, and the characters more exposed to our gaze. This is especially important for those interested in leadership, because in fiction, and particularly the stories included here, we come to see how the situations that people get themselves into are seldom a matter of mere happenstance, but are intimately connected to the kinds of people they are. At the same time, who they become is revealed as bound up in their circumstances. How much more satisfying this is, than the dry lists of leadership skills and virtues with which we are all too often regaled!

FOREWORD

Readers will enjoy this selection of classic texts all the more if they engage in a conversation with Peter Villiers, whose insight and decisive views make for the best kind of conversation.

This short text will be followed by a more extensive survey in the field, to be edited by Peter Villiers and myself. In the latter work, fifteen widely-ranging authors will be examined by the same number of commentators, and some general conclusions drawn. In the meantime, we hope you will enjoy this short and thought-provoking voyage of discovery.

INTRODUCTION

The aim of this book is a simple one. It is to help you, the reader, to perform more effectively in the area that is of importance to you, whether as leader or follower. On occasion, you will need to be able to operate effectively in either role; and the lessons you have learned about leadership will also apply to the practice of its apparent opposite. You will act, in effect, as a reflective practitioner. This book is intended to enlarge the area on which you will be able to reflect, to include not only your own experience but that of others. Those others include people who, by definition, never really existed. They are the product of the sympathetic imagination of the writer.

Who really influenced your ideas on leadership—how to lead, how to be a good leader, how to do it better? And how to cope with the difficulties of leadership: the stresses, the demands, the betrayals and the failure?

We pick up ideas on leadership everywhere, not only from our own experience as both leaders and followers at home, at school, at work and at leisure, but from the experiences of other people of which we learn at second hand. Fiction is a fertile source of that learning, and an inexhaustible source of challenges to us. Novelists, short story writers, playwrights and poets address leadership issues in such a way as to greatly expand the reader's awareness of what it is to be a leader, and how to cope with the difficulties—physical, emotional, intellectual and spiritual—that must arise.

Sometimes the example seems so strong as to be almost first hand—as if the people in a play, a story, a novel, had become part of *our* experience, and we had shared their lives. (John McCain, when a prisoner of war in Vietnam, imagined that his fictional hero, Robert Jordan, was in the cell beyond his own: and his inspiration was not unique.) It need not be great fiction to achieve this. Thrillers can do it: so can comedies, pulp fiction and romance. But it is a mark of good writing that the characters are individuals and not caricatures or stereotypes, and that there is an aspect of the universal to what is portrayed.

INTRODUCTION

Leadership is about learning. How did we learn to be leaders? And how did we learn to be followers? We began at home, and then at school; and those lessons will always be with us, if they need to be revisited, re-assessed, and re-learned as our life progresses. **Rudyard Kipling** revisited his own school-days in *Stalky and Co;* a tale of boarding school and what three dissatisfied and rebellious adolescents learned there. What they absorbed was not on the official curriculum, and the lesson we explore in depth is Kipling's rejection of indoctrination—in this case, the preaching of patriotism. Kipling is a great iconoclast, and is always worth revisiting. We have done so.

Most people, we would guess, have some acquaintance with the works of **William Shakespeare**, even if they have never sat through one of his plays. His characters are so well-known as to be part of our collective imagination, and his language is a substantial part of our own. If we refer to Henry V, Mark Anthony, Julius Caesar or Macbeth, it is at least as likely that the reader will assume that we have Shakespeare's character in mind, as the real historical personage on whom that theatrical creation was based; and our view of history itself has to some extent been shaped by Shakespeare, rather than by any non-theatrical historical account.

We had considered examining some of Shakespeare's leaders in our second chapter, which would have looked at both *Henry V* and *Hamlet*; but wiser counsel prevailed. Shakespeare is a universal writer, and every aspect of leadership is explored in his plays. He deserves a book of his own, but it is not one that we are competent to write, and it would have distorted this text.

Reluctant to abandon him altogether, we have left our comments on the bard to our conclusion, where we briefly examine why Hamlet found himself unable to assume the mantle of leadership when he needed to do so, and was poisoned by the subtle tincture of doubt before the real poison administered by his evil uncle brought an end to the brief and unhappy life of the Prince of Denmark.

Are we entitled to offer our comments on a text, which has not been included in the body of this work as a whole? We think so, for it has enabled us to make a series of comparisons and analogies between the problems faced by Hamlet and those of any contemporary decision-maker, and thus to serve the underlying purpose of this book.

If Hamlet was reluctant to act, then 'Wolf' Larsen is his opposite. **Jack London** shows us the man of action *in extremis*. Larsen is a ship's captain who recognises no limits to his powers or ambitions. He has gorged on Nietzsche, and he is the superman. It is his destiny to command, and for others, like the effete Humphrey van Weyden or the independent-minded Maud Brewster, to obey his commands; for he has the strength of the strong. Larsen is not a mindless thug but the advocate of a new morality; and his ship, the *Ghost*, is the setting for the working-out of that creed. London, a self-made man in every sense, was at one time the most popular writer in the world, and his tales have enthralled and delighted millions. What did he really believe about leadership, and what are the abiding lessons of *The Sea Wolf*?

Ernest Hemingway writes of courage as grace under pressure, and his young hero of the Spanish civil war, Robert Jordan, is full of grace. *'For Whom the Bell Tolls'* is an honest book by an honest writer: a man of letters who pretended to be a man of action. Hemingway is the 'man's man' who is in reality a writer for everyone. It is not our intention to explore in detail, in this short volume, the works of literature that have been especially influential on current leaders. That would be an interesting study, but would make for a very much longer book! However, we may mention in passing that the two opposing candidates for the US presidency in 2008, Barack Obama and John McCain, were both devotees of Hemingway's work, and both acknowledged that it had influenced their ideas on leadership. How did Robert Jordan face up to his difficulties, as a volunteer fighting in another country's war? How was he able to overcome the treachery and defeatism that he encountered? To whom, or to what, did he owe his loyalty? The lessons here do not only apply to war.

Joseph Conrad was a pessimist about both human nature and the possibilities of political achievement. There is, however, a pervasive irony to *The Secret Agent* and a sardonic humour to its style which make this book a delight to read. If it is satirical about the quality of leadership within the British police service (and governmental circles) in combating anarchist 'outrages', then it is a comparatively gentle satire which admires what it mocks and recognises that the best counter to anarchist terrorism is to continue to practise the virtues of toleration, good sense, and restraint that the terrorist finds so irritating.

Leadership, implies Conrad, is a flawed enterprise; but it may still be practised well or badly. The main leader is in this case the assistant commissioner in overall charge of the special crimes section. He cannot trust his main subordinate, a certain chief inspector Heat, to keep him fully informed of what he needs to know: and he must be careful that he is not out-manoeuvred by the machinations and manipulations of others both below and above him in the chain of command. The assistant commissioner, however, does not object to or resent any of this; for it is in the nature of a bureaucracy that information will not be shared. *The Secret Agent* shows us leadership at work in an environment in which nothing is what it seems and no-one is fit to be fully trusted; but in which some objectives are still achieved.

Conrad, a Pole born in the Ukraine who was officially a Russian subject until he obtained British nationality in 1886, wrote as an exile and with an exile's understanding. Captain Konrad Korzeniowski (his original name) had become a master mariner in the British merchant service in the same year as he obtained a British passport; but he could never become an English gentleman. Like Kipling, Conrad understood and could write convincingly about a type and a class to which he himself did not fully belong: for a writer is always an outsider.

George Orwell was born, as he put it himself, into the upper lower middle class, and never lost the voice and manner of an English gentleman. His early years were conventional enough: preparatory school, a scholarship to Eton, and an enlistment in the Imperial Indian Police. Somewhere along the line, however, this privileged young man became a rebel. He reinvented himself as a writer, embraced what he called democratic socialism, and turned a thoughtful eye upon the society that surrounded him. Having seen colonialism from the inside, as it were, he thought it a rotten sham; and he was to express a similar independence of outlook in other circumstances, whilst never losing his belief in the essential decency of humanity. In *Homage to Catalonia*, Orwell recorded the civil war within the Spanish Civil War, in which the communists attacked the anarchists. His work is more an exploration of the nature of politics than of war, and he seems pessimistic about political leadership in almost any context.

Orwell was an enemy not of communism but of totalitarianism, and although he declared himself a socialist he was fundamentally a libertarian. He believed in the freedom to be odd, eccentric or even self-destructive (as he showed in his own life) so long as one did not exploit others (as he had done as an imperial policeman); and like Joseph Conrad, he was a disbeliever in utopias.

In *Animal Farm*, Orwell presented so devastating a satire on the failed utopia of the Soviet Union (thinly disguised as an allegory) that the publisher's reader T S Elliott refused to publish it in wartime, as damaging to the British ally Joseph Stalin. In *Nineteen Eighty-Four* Orwell goes further and presents a wholly bleak vision of a future world in which the past has been erased and Big Brother controls the party through surveillance and propaganda and the proles—the unskilled working class, or proletariat in Karl Marx's term—by mindless entertainment. Not only is the future bereft of hope: it is brutal, ugly and soulless. Leadership, in Orwell's writings, is not a neutral element. It can be a force for good or evil. But evil tends to prevail, and the leader who manipulates language itself is the ultimate threat. Orwell's 'science fiction' remains all too relevant to the world around us, and his hope for leadership as decency is enduring.

R C Sherriff is a quintessentially English writer who shows us a different aspect of grace under pressure. In his play *Journey's End*, we are in a dugout in the Great War in the spring of 1918, and the Germans are about to launch a devastating attack. The whisky-sodden but resolute company commander, Captain Stanhope, fears that the attack will succeed, but he is still determined that he and his men will do their duty. He has been in the trenches for three years, all of his friends have been killed, and he does not fear death for himself; indeed, he rather welcomes the prospect of ending his lonely existence and rejoining the company of the dead. His conflict lies elsewhere.

The real conflict in the dugout, and the real challenge to Stanhope's leadership, is not the impending battle, but the arrival of a new, young officer who knew Stanhope before the war, when Stanhope was his hero at school; and Stanhope had an 'understanding' with his sister. Raleigh presents a challenge that the tough, drink-sodden, company commander cannot resolve; and when his only confidante, his second-in-command who is called 'Uncle', is killed in a suicidal raid on the German position which has been ordered by headquarters, Stanhope has almost reached his journey's end. This is an immensely powerful and moving drama, conveyed with understatement and humour, which explores the contrast between image and reality and tests the foundations of leadership to the point of destruction, but does not destroy them altogether. Hope exists, even at a time of Armageddon; for the human spirit will survive.

Conclusion: The enduring leader

We shall finish with a brief comment on *Jane Eyre*, by Charlotte Bronte, as a perfect study in leadership through resilience. Jane, small, plain, and in every sense underprivileged, has had a miserable start in life. Left an orphan, she is cheated out of her potential inheritance by an embittered aunt. She barely survives her inadequate education in an appalling school, in which her only friend, Helen Burns, dies of tuberculosis—a death that could easily have been prevented. Jane becomes a teacher in her own right; and finally she leaves school and enters adult life to become a governess at Thornfield Hall.

Still small and plain, if by now fully self-aware and fully able to think and act for herself, Jane proves more than a match for the master of the house, Mr Rochester, who finds it impossible to impose his will upon her, and finally falls in love and proposes. However, he is already married!—his insane and dangerous wife is imprisoned in the attic. Jane leaves in haste, and spends many months elsewhere. When she is finally drawn back (having come into her inheritance as a result of her wicked aunt's deathbed repentance) she finds the hall burned down, Mr Rochester's wife dead as a result of the fire—and Mr Rochester blinded. Soon follows one of the most famous lines in English literature:

INTRODUCTION

Reader, I married him.

Jane triumphs: but it is not the triumph of a plaster saint whose faith has effortlessly allowed her to overcome any adversity. Jane forgives her enemies, in her own way. She rises above the wrongs that they have heaped upon her: from the aunt who cheated her of her inheritance; to the staff at the school who neglected their duties and damaged the children under their care; and to Mr Rochester himself, who had somehow neglected to tell his even-tempered young governess that he was already married. Jane rises above all of this. She forgives; but at the same time she preserves her authenticity. Jane is not a saint, but someone who does not wish to be damaged goods. She is an ordinary young woman with an extraordinary strength of character; and she leads not by exhortation but by example. She remains in the reader's mind long after her story is over; and she is with us still.

Robert Jordan is scratching the date on the wall in the next cell, and dreaming of freedom.

Wolf Larsen is trapped in his disintegrating body, while his mind remains active.

Harvey Cheyne, Junior, the former ship's boy in Kipling's *Captains Courageous*, has achieved his destiny as a captain of industry. He is looking back with nostalgia on his early days at sea, when the challenges faced by a leader were simpler, at least in memory.

Winston Smith, the victim of a soulless future in *Nineteen-Eighty Four*, has bought his old-fashioned notebook from a shop-keeper who will prove to be an agent of the thought police, and is making his first entry: he has yet to embark upon his illicit love affair with Julia which the thought police will use to destroy him.

Captain Dennis Stanhope, the company commander of *Journey's End*, is about to carry out his final duty—and without the whisky that has so far sustained him. He has made peace with Raleigh, the reminder of his youth; and the shells are exploding in the trench outside the dugout.

Conrad's assistant commissioner lives on in his unhappy marriage, his consolation the exercise of his professional skills. Chief Inspector

Heat is slightly less convinced of his infallibility; and the Professor continues his lonely patrol of the shabbier streets of the Metropolis, his hand grasping the India-rubber ball by which he may at any moment destroy himself and those around him.

Hamlet is already dead: he was unable to cope with the pressures that his uncle's villainy and his mother's infidelity brought upon him, and the poison which was administered by deception has proved a release from mental torment.

Jane Eyre, however, is with us still. She is the companion who is both solace and delight to her husband and a constant provocation to his limitations. She is the patient, careful, authoritative school-teacher who is moulding our future citizens to be decent and honourable men and women, who know what it means to keep their word. She is the leader who knows the frailties of human nature, and has never allowed them to vanquish her aspirations. Jane lives.

CHAPTER 1

Where East Meets West: Rudyard Kipling

If you can talk with crowds and keep your virtue,
Or walk with kings - nor lose the common touch;
If neither foes nor loving friends can hurt you;
If all men count with you, but none too much;
If you can fill the unforgiving minute
With sixty seconds' worth of distance run -
Yours is the Earth and everything that's in it,
And — which is more — you'll be a Man my son!

From 'If'

Rudyard Kipling was born in India in 1865 of English parents, and went on to make his reputation as a writer of Indian tales and poems, just as Joseph Conrad made his as a teller of tales of the sea. Both men outgrew their origins: but it is as a writer of India under the Raj that Kipling is mainly remembered. The Jungle Book has a universal appeal, and remains popular with Mr Disney—an outcome which, we suspect, Mr Kipling himself would have regarded with an ironic approval. Kipling's poem 'If' was voted the most popular poem in the English language in a BBC poll conducted in 1995. What is the appeal of this writer, whose attitudes were formed under Queen Victoria? Why has it lasted? And what does his literature have to tell us about leadership?

George Orwell, who had also been born of English parents in India, wrote a highly perceptive essay about Kipling and his imperial background and attitudes (Orwell, 1942). Orwell's attitude to Kipling was ambivalent, as Meyers points out in his perceptive biography (Meyers, 2000, page 267). On the one hand, Orwell hated imperialism—in which he had participated as an imperial police officer in Burma—and despised Kipling as an apologist for empire. On the other hand, he admired Kipling for his recognition of the reality of empire and

CHAPTER 1

his sense of responsibility. Both Orwell and Kipling despised what would now be called the chattering classes, whom Orwell described as pansies, and Kipling attacked as mocking the uniforms that guarded them while they slept. Moreover, there was something enduring about Kipling. As Orwell wrote in 1942:

> 'During five literary generations every enlightened person has despised (Kipling), and at the end of that time nine-tenths of those enlightened persons are forgotten and Kipling is in some sense still there.'

Was Kipling a committed imperialist, and (almost necessarily) a racist to boot? And if he were, does that mean that we can learn nothing from his writings? Orwell said that he was, but did not deny that we could. Kipling was a product of his time and accepted the prevailing mores. However, his poetry is an inexhaustible source of quotations which may be interpreted to support a variety of attitudes. In his own way, Kipling was proud of what the British had achieved, and supported the imperial mission. He made fun of babus—semi-educated Indian clerks, with a penchant for pretentious expression—and he was convinced that Anglo-Saxons made good administrators, even if they were not also literary men. But his prejudices did not blind him, and we may still appreciate his work. Perhaps we shall find out more of his core values as we explore his life and writing in a little more detail, and uncover his views on leadership.

Kipling's life and times

Rudyard Kipling's parents were both well-educated and well-connected but were not well-off. Rudyard lived in Bombay, where his father worked, until he was six; and his early upbringing had a profound influence upon him, for according to his own account he learned to speak Hindu with the family servants before he had mastered English. As was the custom, his sister and he were sent back to England to be educated, and Kipling spent the next six years in the care of a loathsome couple in Southsea, who bullied him unmercifully.

CHAPTER 1

His mother visited England in 1877, found out what was happening, and took him away forthwith: and he was sent to board at the United Services College in Westward Ho!, Devon.

Despite its impressive name, this was far from being one of the leading public schools. But it was affordable, and it had an impressive head master, John Cormell Price, on whom Kipling bases the sympathetic headmaster of his book Stalky & Co. Cormell Price, who had artistic connexions and was a friend of the Kipling family, was not a typical headmaster. He had been appointed to head a school that made the military crammer unnecessary, since it would provide the coaching necessary for the army entrance examination. He did so, but was also determined to make it a proper place of learning. Kipling was to remain in touch with his old headmaster until Cormell Price's death in 1910, and to be greatly influenced by him.

Kipling throve at boarding school, despite his inability at games (short, strongly built, and very short-sighted, he went by the nick-name of gig-lamps, in honour of his spectacles). In Stalky & Co., which is clearly based on his own experience, he is very much the junior member of a rebellious triumvirate, whose fictitious names are Stalky, M'Turk and Beetle, and who do their best to undermine the authority of those of the senior boys and masters whom they do not respect, usually by guile and deception rather than by outright revolt. They are nevertheless susceptible to the appeal of true authority as represented by the headmaster, whom they respect as being straight, with no pretence or hypocrisy, and who recognises their individuality and nurtures their cultural interests.

At school, Kipling discovered a passion for literature in general and for poetry in particular, and began to write his own, as well as editing the college magazine under the watchful eye of the head. His future was clearly as a writer, and he left school at sixteen and went out to rejoin his family in India, where his father Lockwood Kipling was now Principal of the Mayo College of Art and Curator of the Lahore Museum. Despite having blighted his early youth by dumping him in Southsea, Kipling's parents loved their son and understood his needs. Kipling needed to write; and he became the assistant editor of the Civil and Military Gazette in Lahore.

CHAPTER 1

Over the next seven years Kipling showed an astonishing combination of talent and dedication, and his gifts were immediately recognised. He soaked up information like a sponge, and wrote verse or prose as easily as he breathed. He took his duties as an assistant editor seriously and they gave him an extraordinary insight into the doings of what was in effect a multi-racial and multi-cultural society, even if the British were officially on top. He travelled, he investigated, he reported, and he had dealings with men and women of all backgrounds and races: for if Kipling was an imperialist he was never a snob. Short, dark, and heavily moustachioed, he might have been Indian or part-Indian himself: and he found life in India far too interesting to be over-identified with one particular race or culture.

Kim

Part of the charm of his sole Indian novel, Kim, which Prime Minister Nehru of India was to describe as his favourite book, is that the eponymous Kim sees and understands Indian society neither as ruler nor underdog, but as a free spirit who is not constrained by his social or racial background. Kim—Kimball O'Hara—is the orphaned son of an Irish sergeant, who is brought up by an Indian woman. Although white, he knows India and its peoples as if he were a native. He becomes the chela (servant) of a Tibetan monk, and at the same time proves a natural in intelligence work for the Indian Secret Service, by whom he is fostered as a long-term investment: for Kim, the white youth who can easily pass himself off as an Indian, is suited both by background and temperament to such work. It fascinates him, and he enjoys the drama involved, to the extent that at one point he wonders who is the real Kim: a not unknown dilemma for an intelligence agent.

Kim shows Kipling's love of India in all its vastness and complexity. The Indian and Tibetan characters in the story are well-drawn, and the story as a whole is conspicuous for its absence of racial prejudice: unless it be a prejudice against (or perhaps it might be called a justified dislike for) the white colonialist who has no interest in the Indians and their history, culture and traditions. Kim is far happier in his Indian persona than as a conventional sahib, whose habits are seen (and mocked) through Indian eyes; and the Englishmen to whom he is drawn are men like Colonel Creighton or Lurgan Sahib, who have identified themselves fully with India and its peoples, whilst not pretending to be Indians themselves. Like them, and indeed like Kipling himself, Kim accepts that at heart he is a chela of the Raj; and that if his talents impel him towards a life of deception, his fundamental loyalty is clear.

Kim was published in 1901, long after its author had left India. The young Rudyard Kipling had published his first book of verse in 1886 as a railway book, and his first selection of short stories, Plain Tales from the Hills, in the same year. Six more collections of short stories soon followed, and by the age of 22 Kipling was already a recognised and successful author. It was time to leave India and make his reputation in London, the capital of the empire and its literary Everest; and he was only to return to India for one brief visit.

Kipling conquered his British Everest, for this brash young upstart had a genius that could not be ignored. He married an American named Caroline Balestier, having proposed to her by telegram. They lived in Vermont from 1892 to 1896 before returning to England, where he did his best to avoid the publicity which attached itself to a famous writer: although he was always happy to talk to children. The Kiplings had three children of their own, and his life seemed to be becoming ever more productive and successful. In 1907, he was the youngest recipient of the Nobel Prize for Literature, and his reputation was at its peak. He was still only 42.

Sadness had, however, intervened. His beloved older daughter died at ten, his marriage became less spontaneous, and finally his son Jack was killed in the trenches in the Great War—a death for which his father must have felt not only sorrow but guilt, for he had engineered a commission in the Irish Guards for a boy who was, like his father, desperately short-sighted, and in a physical sense, unfit to serve.

With a declining popularity, but still an enormous following—rather like the empire to which he remained true—Kipling continued to write until his death in 1936 at his sombre mansion of 'Batemans', where he had resided for 32 years. His reputation has plunged and soared since his death, and it is possible both to love and hate his work at the same time.

Kipling on the development of leadership in adolesence

Kipling wrote both for adults and children, and had a particular insight into the challenges and trials of childhood and adolescence. In this chapter we explore his views on how the capacity to lead is developed in early manhood. To do that we shall briefly examine two of his works, Stalky and Co. and Captains Courageous. One is in effect a collection of short stories, set in a school in Devon; and the other takes place aboard an American fishing schooner on the Grand Banks.

Stalky & Co.

Stalky & Co. is a school story, and an example of Kipling's contribution to an extremely popular genre: the initiation of a young man into maturity through the medium of the public school. This subject began with Tom Brown's Schooldays, by Thomas Hughes (first published in 1857) in which the youthful Thomas Brown is sent to Rugby public school in order to obtain the elements of an education. The headmaster of the real public school which is the setting for the story was also real: Thomas Arnold, a famous headmaster and educator, who was father of the famous poet (and schools inspector) Matthew Arnold. Tom Brown is a gauche, well-meaning and appallingly innocent. He is horribly bullied by the cad Flashman—one of the problems of this book for a later and more cynical readership is that Flashman is an intensely convincing character, which is more than can be said for some of his victims—and is redeemed when about to go off the rails by his innocent love for a sickly new boy, George Arthur, who is placed under his special protection. The book is a good read, if its Victorian sentimentality has not worn well; and it started an avalanche to which Kipling was later to contribute in his own special style.

Stalky & Co. preaches the virtues of rebellion. It suggests that boys are more likely to grow up to be responsible and successful citizens if they are allowed a reasonable latitude in their youth, and are not simply forced to conform. It is important to recognise that they are adolescents: a plant which has not fully grown. Those who are too successful in their youth are unlikely to repeat that success later on; for they have already 'peaked', and life after boarding school does not present the same challenges and rewards as success in a confined and artificial environment. In the same way, those who are too thoroughly crushed will never flourish; and there must be a way forward between the two extremes.

If youth is to rebel, who is there to ensure that the young person does not go off the rails completely, and to provide an example of admirable behaviour? Given that the boarding school youth's parents have already abrogated that responsibility, the remaining choice is limited. At the United Services College, it is the headmaster who provides the model of leadership that the boys require; and it is he, and not the chaplain or any housemaster or current sporting hero who is in both law and estimation, in loco parentis.

The headmaster (who is known in the story as Bates, or Bates Sahib) is the role model for leadership in Stalky & Co. He is an excellent headmaster because he understands boys and accepts them for what they are. He sets standards, maintains discipline and upholds the authority of his masters and prefects; but he is never vindictive, oppressive or unfair. Perhaps most important of all, he has a sense of humour. His virtues can be seen in every chapter. Here we shall explore a little more closely an episode in which his opposite is presented: someone who does not understand boys and who tramples on their aspirations.

The Flag of Their Country

The chapter begins with the older boys at the United Services College more-or-less accidentally beginning to drill seriously, under the guidance of a retired army sergeant nicknamed Foxy. Foxy enforces discipline at the school and has a minor but important role in the book. Foxy is not regarded by the boys as being in authority over them, that position being reserved for the masters. It is his role to develop in

CHAPTER 1

others the leadership qualities that as a former non-commissioned officer he has not been required to exercise himself, but perhaps understands better than their practitioners; and he has both affection and respect for the boys under his charge.

The drill is supposed to lead to the formation of the school's very own army cadet force; but fate intervenes. A politician named Raymond Martin is invited to visit the school. The subject of his speech, of his own choice, is patriotism. The headmaster has accepted him as the friend of a friend, and as soon as he meets Mr Martin he realises that the other, despite his confidence and self-assurance, is unsuited to his task. Dinner is over, and the talk begins.

> 'Mr. Raymond Martin plunged into his speech with a long-drawn, rasping "Well, boys," that, though they were not conscious of it, set every young nerve ajar…

He goes on to say that:

> 'They must remember that they would not always be boys. They would grow up into men, because the boys of to-day made the men of to-morrow, and upon the men of to-morrow the fair fame of their glorious native land depended…

Kipling comments:

> 'Now the reserve of a boy is tenfold deeper than the reserve of a maid, she being made for one end only by blind Nature, but man for several. With a large and healthy hand, he tore down these veils, and trampled them under the well-intentioned feet of eloquence. In a raucous voice, he cried aloud little matters, like the hope of Honour and the dream of Glory, that boys do not discuss even with their most intimate equals, cheerfully assuming that, till he spoke, they had never considered these possibilities…

> 'And so he worked towards his peroration.'

This was to display the flag of their country. It was greeted in silence.

CHAPTER 1

'... The volunteer cadet-corps fell in next Monday, depressedly, with a face of shame. Even then, judicious silence might have turned the corner.

'Said Foxy: "After a fine speech like what you 'eard night before last, you ought to take 'old of your drill with re-newed activity. I don't see how you can avoid comin' out an' marchin' in the open now."

"Can't we get out of it, then, Foxy?" Stalky's fine old silky tone should have warned him.

"No, not with his giving the flag so generously..."'

'Stalky returned his rifle to the rack in dead silence, and fell out. His example was followed by Hogan and Ansell. Perowne hesitated. "Look here, oughtn't we—?" he began.

"I'll get it out of the locker in a minute," said the Sergeant, his back turned. "Then we can—"

"Come on!" shouted Stalky. "What the devil are you waiting for? Dismiss! Break off."

"Why—what the—where the—?"

'The rattle of Sniders, slammed into the rack, drowned his voice, as boy after boy fell out.

"I—I don't know that I shan't have to report this to the Head," he stammered.

"Report, then, and be damned to you," cried Stalky, white to the lips, and ran out.'

The moral is clear. The head would not have made such a speech. It is unnecessary, since the boys are already patriotic and prepared to die for their country if need be—a prospect that Mr Raymond Martin, MP, the purveyor of ideals at second-hand, does not himself face. As a result, his efforts lead to the end of the drill squad—decided upon, of course, by Stalky, the natural leader, who influences the older boys in their decision—and a vindication of the headmaster's judgment. The United Services College exists, not to promote the spirit of patriotism which is already present in its pupils, but to develop their characters so that they are able to serve their country to good effect. They must be competent servants of an ideal which is never stated but by which they will be judged.

Captains Courageous

Captains Courageous—written and first published in 1903 in America, where Kipling was living with his wife Carrie—has a very different setting. The spoiled young Harvey Cheyne, Jr, the son of an American multi-millionaire and his over-protective wife, falls overboard from a liner and is picked up from the sea by a passing doryman, Manuel. He is taken aboard the fishing schooner We're Here, where the captain's son, Dan Troop, asks him how he fell overboard.

"How'd you come to fall off in a dead flat ca'am?"

"'Twasn't a calm," said Harvey, sulkily. "It was a gale, and I was seasick. Guess I must have rolled over the rail."

"There was a little common swell yes'day an' last night," said the boy. "But ef thet's your notion of a gale——" He whistled. "You'll know more 'fore you're through. Hurry! Dad's waitin'."

Like many other unfortunate young people, Harvey had never in all his life received a direct order—never, at least, without long, and sometimes tearful, explanations of the advantages of obedience and the reasons for the request. Mrs. Cheyne lived in fear of breaking his spirit, which, perhaps, was the reason that she herself walked on the edge of nervous prostration. He could not see why he should be expected to hurry for any man's pleasure, and said so. "Your dad can come down here if he's so anxious to talk to me. I want him to take me to New York right away. It'll pay him."

Dan opened his eyes as the size and beauty of this joke dawned on him. "Say, Dad!" he shouted up the foc's'le hatch, "he says you kin slip down an' see him ef you're anxious that way. 'Hear, Dad?"

CHAPTER 1

The answer came back in the deepest voice Harvey had ever heard from a human chest: "Quit foolin', Dan, and send him to me."

"Mornin'," said Harvey... As one rescued from drowning, (he) expected sympathy. His mother suffered agonies whenever he got his feet wet; but this mariner did not seem excited...

Harvey gave his name, the name of the steamer, and a short history of the accident, winding up with a demand to be taken back immediately to New York...

"I'm grateful enough for being saved and all that, of course! but I want you to understand that the sooner you take me back to New York the better it'll pay you... You've done the best day's work you ever did in your life when you pulled me in. I'm all the son Harvey Cheyne has."

"He's bin favoured," said Disko, dryly.'

Harvey argues on, and insults the ship, and for the second time accuses its master of theft; and the master knocks him down. Having little choice in the matter, Harvey finally accepts his new position: assistant ship's boy, at ten and a half dollars a month, until the ship returns to her home port in New England, several months later.

The voyage that follows is the making of him. The ship and its crew provide everything that his life has lacked until then: work, discipline, responsibility, a shared purpose, and people to admire (role models, in the current phrase: Kipling would have enjoyed mocking it). When the We're Here finally returns to her home port of Gloucester, Massachusetts, Harvey's parents can hardly recognize him, for the spoiled adolescent has become a man.

His father is both pleased and impressed, whereas his mother is perhaps a little wistful for the boy who has gone (and, perhaps, the role she has lost.) Harvey Cheyne, Senior, then in effect decides his son's further development for him; firstly, he will obtain a proper college education, so that he can compete on equal terms with other magnates; and then he will assume responsibility for part of his father's empire.

CHAPTER 1

His son is happy with this (as who would not be?) and lays down a marker: he wishes to take charge of the tea-clippers that his father has recently acquired as part of a larger business deal. His father agrees; and, always the controller, he also agrees with Disko Troop that his son Dan can become an apprentice on a tea-clipper, with a view to eventual command. The black, Gaelic-speaking cook of the We're Here decides to follow Harvey's star; and everyone, with the possible exception of Mrs Cheyne, who now has no-one to mother, is happy.

Does the story ring true? Partly. The older Cheyne is presented favourably by the author, and we may infer that Kipling admires initiative and enterprise and expects businessmen to be ruthless in seizing an advantage; and Harvey Cheyne, Senior represents for Kipling the founding of the American west. Harvey Cheyne tells his son the story of his own life 'in a low, even voice, without gesture and without expression...

> 'It covered the building of three railroads and the deliberate wreck of a fourth. It told of steamers, townships, forests, and mines, and the men of every nation under heaven, manning, creating, hewing, and digging these. It touched on chances of gigantic wealth flung before eyes that could not see, or missed by the merest accident of time and travel; and through the mad shift of things, sometimes on horseback, more often afoot, now rich, now poor, in and out, and back and forth, deck-hand, train-hand, contractor, boarding-house keeper, journalist, engineer, drummer, real-estate agent, politician, dead-beat, rum-seller, mine-owner, speculator, cattle-man, or tramp, moved Harvey Cheyne, alert and quiet, seeking his own ends, and, so he said, the glory and advancement of his country.
>
> 'He told of the faith that never deserted him even when he hung on the ragged edge of despair—the faith that comes of knowing men and things... The tale held Harvey almost breathless, his head a little cocked to one side, his eyes fixed on his father's face, as the twilight deepened and the red cigar-end lit up the furrowed cheeks and heavy eyebrows. It seemed to him like watching a locomotive storming across country in the dark...'

The We're Here presents a learning environment in which the young Harvey must serve his apprenticeship and learn to obey others before he can command men for himself; and that is an invaluable experience. It is not his background that counts, but what he is, in himself. He begins the story as a spoiled adolescent, and ends it as a young man who has demonstrated the potential for leadership.

Kipling's views on leadership

In Kipling's view, if we are to judge from the values which appear to underly most of his fiction, leadership is a masculine preoccupation. Girls and women are largely irrelevant to man's business. They are not expected to become leaders, but to produce them: therefore, they need not be prepared for the responsibility of leadership themselves.

After gender comes race. The Anglo-Saxon is more likely to be a good investment, other things being equal. Other whites are not quite the same. Celts tend to be 'fey', and therefore fulfill a mystical role—as does the black cook of the We're Here, who has mastered the Gaelic and is therefore an honorary Celt.[1] Manuel the doryman, who saves Harvey Cheyne from drowning, is a Portuguese and therefore he is happy-go-lucky in his approach to life, attractive to women (not necessarily an asset in the Anglo-Saxon view), someone who shows a childlike devotion to the role of the Roman Catholic church, and so on. He might make a good nco; but, like Foxy, he is not officer material.

Leadership, in Kipling's world, is essentially a duty, and is not undertaken in the hope of material prosperity or wider recognition. Most of his examples come from empire; and although these men may be inspired by ideals of some sort, they do not articulate them. The imperial army officer, engineer, doctor or administrator (or the journalist that Kipling became) has an ideal of service: but, unlike the right honourable Raymond Martin. M.P., he does not proselytize about it. He is neither propagandist nor intellectual. His artistic interests are severely limited. His interest in other cultures is non-existent, for he has no real knowledge of his own. His education at boarding school has trained him to lead an austere and self-denying existence, in which a little tennis or rough shooting, with the occasional evening at the club, is all the relaxation that he needs. He is at home within a disciplined and ordered environment, and he believes that is his task to bring a form of civilization (to India or elsewhere) of which the natives are very much in need—even if they do not recognize it for themselves. Above all, he does not question the status quo; for it is his job to make it work.

The leadership paradox

Kipling's views appear at first glance to be entirely conventional. It would seem that the exercise of leadership (in the imperial context, at least) is the prerogative of white, male candidates from an almost hereditary officer class. Officers emerge from the preparatory and public school system which is designed to produce them, and are usually white Anglo-Saxon Protestants (WASPs.) To be born a WASP is therefore an (almost) necessary but not a sufficient qualification for leadership; for the future leader has to be 'socialized.' Potential leaders show obedience. They accept the authority of those placed in charge of them and work willingly to serve the community. They respond well to discipline, and are not noted for their originality. They are athletes rather than aesthetes; they do not go into things too deeply; and they have a wholesome regard for the established order, which may tolerate eccentricity but not disloyalty.

That may be all very well: but we may immediately note two incongruities. Firstly, Kipling himself was not a good example of the cast he supposedly admired. Although he had not gone to university and had no academic pretensions, he was highly intelligent and articulate, with a very strong interest in the arts. Two of his aunts were married to famous painters, his mother and sister were artistically inclined, and his father, Lockwood Kipling, was a professor of arts and crafts who was determined to ensure that India preserved its cultural heritage against foreign invasion. Lockwood Kipling was both an imperialist and a paternalist in his approach to his work: but he had an encyclopedic knowledge of India and its crafts. He shared that interest with his son, with whom he established a working partnership. Neither was an unthinking imperialist; and Rudyard Kipling was very far indeed from the classic imperial 'type' (as, for example, later satirized by a young George Orwell in his first novel, Burmese Days.) He was too clever; he was too quick-witted; and he was too sure of his abilities. Moreover, he was to show himself capable of writing Kim.

Secondly, the public school virtues that we have outlined are not the qualities shown by Stalky and Co. Those three potential leaders are selfish, cunning and devious. They do not accept the mores of the public school system, and their outright rebelliousness is only just kept in check by a highly resourceful headmaster, who has frequent recourse to corporal punishment—and who gives 'Beetle'—Kipling's nick-name for himself in this semi-autobiographical work— the run of his library. Notwithstanding this, however, all three complete their school careers and go on to success in later life, Stalky in particular becoming a general and a great leader of men.

The message of Stalky & Co. is clear. The true leader is a rebel: or rather, he needs a period of rebelliousness as an adolescent, in which he may challenge the system, find his own values, and decide what is really important to him. That rebellion, however, needs to take place in a disciplined environment which contains role models for good behaviour. Self-made men like Harvey Cheyne, Senior, who rebel against their beginning in life, may be admired for their drive and determination; but there is something a little too egotistical and dogmatic about the self-made man, and their sons must be educated and civilized before they can exercise proper leadership.

Is that it, then? Far from it; for there is more to Kipling than first meets the eye, as his novel Kim demonstrates. His poem 'If' suggests that resilience is the key ingredient of manhood (and hence of leadership); and we finish with another quatrain by Rudyard Kipling, the arch-conservative and poet of empire.

> *Oh, East is East and West is West, and never the twain shall meet,*
> *Till Earth and Sky stand presently at God's great Judgment Seat;*
> *But there is neither East nor West, Border, nor Breed, nor Birth,*
> *When two strong men stand face to face, tho' they come from the ends of the earth.*

Questions for reflection

In regard to the questions that follow, readers are encouraged to reflect upon their own experiences, outlook, and general views, as well as whatever they may have gained from reading Rudyard Kipling.

- Is adolescence a natural time for rebellion?

- Do future leaders need a period in which they can challenge the customs and conventions that surround them? Why?

- Is it necessary to learn to obey, before one can command?

- Rudyard Kipling is indelibly associated with British India, and clearly approved of imperialism. Is his writing still relevant to-day? How?

Commentary on questions

The questions which follow each chapter do not have model answers, but are designed to encourage reflection, either by one reader working alone or as a member of a discussion group.

In the latter case, the questions may well serve as a prompt to wider discussion. If you are approaching these questions as a prompt to group discussion, please be sure to decide beforehand how far you want to go, in terms of disclosure. Naturally, the more that you reveal about yourself and your experiences of leadership, whether as practitioner or recipient, the more you (and others) may gain from the discussion. However, it may be sensible to agree some rules about confidentiality in advance. Sticking to generalities is safe but boring. Personal revelation can be exciting but dangerous. We suggest that you find the middle way!

Another and perhaps an additional way to make use of these questions is to follow them up on our website, of which details are provided at the end of the book.

☐ Is adolescence a natural time for rebellion?

This is a difficult question (hence its inclusion), and one's views on this may depend at least in part on one's own background and cultural heritage. It is, perhaps, received wisdom in 'western' societies that adolescents will tend to be rebellious, and that this is a necessary part of growing up: but this may not be a universal assumption. Societies and cultures differ. In some societies children 'grow up' very much faster than in others; and attitudes to authority vary.

Adolescence offers the opportunity for rebellion, in a way that childhood and maturity do not; and many commentators, the conservatively minded Sir Winston Churchill included, have said that it is natural that adolescents should be questioning or even radical whilst developing their own views. To be questioning or radical in one's thought is not necessarily to be rebellious: but the distinction is a subtle one. An insight into adolescence is offered in the title (and content) of what was perhaps James Dean's most famous film: 'Rebel without a Cause.'

☐ Do future leaders need a period in which they can challenge the customs and conventions that surround them? Why?

This author believes that they do, but would find it hard to explain quite why. It has something to do with being able to step back in order to progress further. The person who is a little too ready to conform, to learn the rules, and to find his place in an established order may well prove to be a reliable and dependable functionary in an organised framework, but is less likely to show the originality of mind and the capacity to challenge and improve upon perceived wisdom which are amongst the hallmarks of the true leader.

It is not true that only a maverick makes a good leader; and there are dangers to the practice of 'charismatic leadership' which have been clearly identified, for example by Michael Maccoby in a powerfully written article in the Harvard Business Review (Maccoby, 2000.) Maccoby addresses what he calls narcissistic leaders, but there is a

CHAPTER 1

strong overlap to what is normally described as charismatic leadership. (The word 'charisma' has been overused, and its original connotation is a religious one; but it has a recognised meaning in everyday speech.)

'Charismatic' leaders, who dominate others by force of personality, can be exciting to be around; but their practice of leadership, which favours risk-taking and the rejection of established methods of operating, may be dangerous.

A period of reflection is not only useful to future leaders. Many leaders and managers who are already in post may benefit from an opportunity for reflection, and the opportunity to challenge the customs and conventions that surround them, once they have gathered some inside knowledge of the organisation in which they operate. Indeed, the desire for such an opportunity may have been a part of your motivation in buying this book!

- Is it necessary to learn to obey, before one can command?

Again, the author believes that the answer is yes, although he is not quite sure how to explain why.

It is received wisdom in the armed services that someone who has been selected as a future officer should learn to obey before he can command others; but that axiom may not apply in other organisations. In any case an organisation such as the army requires that all its members should obey orders instantly on occasion, even if those orders should seem dangerous or nonsensical. Obedience, in other words, is an essential part of military life, and is usually reinforced by the use or threat of discipline. Even a traditional military organisation will acknowledge, however, that true discipline should come from within.

The issue of obedience arises in Ernest Hemingway's novel For Whom the Bell Tolls, which is explored in depth later in this volume. Robert Jordan, the unofficial leader of a guerrilla group engaged in fighting superior forces in the Spanish civil war, needs to know that his followers will obey his orders: but he does not have the reassurance of formal military discipline to reinforce his commands. It is of great interest, therefore, to discover how he does enforce obedience, which is largely by the exertion of what might be called moral authority. It is also clear that although he has no formal status in his guerrilla group, he is in some way part of a chain of command that stretches above them, to the directors of the republican cause in general. However, I am beginning to discuss another chapter which you will not yet have read, and must impose some discipline upon my comments!

> ☐ Rudyard Kipling is indelibly associated with British India, and clearly approved of imperialism. Is his writing still relevant to-day? How?

All writers must, by definition, be a product of their time and circumstances: but that is not all that they are. The writer is a free spirit, and his aim is to find the truth, rather than unthinkingly either to support or attack the values to which he was introduced in childhood or adolescence. He may not find the whole truth; but it is a measure of his greatness as a writer that he is able, at least to some extent, to distance himself from the prejudices of his own background and circumstances, and to reach out for the universal. In doing so, he must create a story and characters that are convincing in themselves, whatever his own background or views; and we, the readers, must wish to continue reading that story because we care about the people in it, and we want to know what happens to them.

Commentators refer to the universality of Shakespeare because his works address the human condition as a whole. Shakespeare was able, not only to efface himself and his own views from his works, but almost to efface himself altogether. Shakespeare lives on through his published work; but despite the huge number of books that have been written about him, very little is known for certain about his life, and nothing of his own views. Does the person who enjoys his plays, need to know what Shakespeare 'really' thought about marriage, or adultery, or regicide? Does the theatre-goer or play-reader need to know whether or not Shakespeare approved of his characters, or what they did or didn't do? To pose such questions is to point to their absurdity. To know something about the background and circumstances of a writer may help the reader to understand more about their work, and thus to gain more from it; but that knowledge is neither necessary nor sufficient for the work to be appreciated. Writers are judged by what they produce, and not by their lives, and are thus the opposite of celebrities.

Kipling was a lesser writer than Shakespeare, and was less successful in erasing himself from his work—which included journalism as well as fiction. One may already know that Kipling was an imperialist, because he advocated imperialism in his non-fictional work. Similarly, one may already know that Kipling was absorbed by British India, because that was the society that surrounded him when he began to write his short stories, and the source of the raw material that he needed. That does not entitle one to infer that Kipling was devoted heart and soul to the empire, or that he simply saw himself as its apologist; and if his works were too obviously designed to support the imperial cause, they might be classified as more propaganda than literature.

A good writer is read by people who may agree with, reject, or be indifferent to his political views, in so far as they may be inferred from the text: and a novel or play which sets up easy targets so that the author may then knock them down is not serving the purpose of literature. There is a difference between characterisation and caricature, and a work of fiction is not the same thing as an essay or a tract. The test of a good writer is not that his works advocate the right political solutions, but that they are still being read.

CHAPTER 2

The Sea Wolf: Jack London

Jack London (1876-1916) died as he had lived, to excess. In committing suicide he used two poisons which worked against each other, with the result that his death agony was a prolonged one. Or so wrote his early biographer, Irving Stone (Stone, 1938); for there was something larger than life about Jack London, and it was hard to believe he had died an ordinary death.

Jack London died a hopeless alcoholic, whose first marriage had failed and whose second marriage had not produced the son for whom he hoped. He had written himself out. He was heavily in debt, and had taken on commitments that he could not possibly fulfill, for his ambitions were always greater than even his remarkable achievements. His sailing schooner, the Snark, which he had designed himself, had proved an embarrassingly expensive failure; and his plans for his ranch in California were equally unsuccessful. He had invested large sums of money in advanced agricultural schemes, rather than sticking to what was tried and tested. Finally, a fire consumed his magnificent ranch building, Wolf House, which was intended to last 1000 years, and reduced it to ashes.

Although he had attended college for a short period, London had never graduated. He had never made a success of his political ambitions, which were in any case contradictory; and he had never really mastered the art of constructing a novel, as his critics did not tire of pointing out.

He was, nevertheless, the most successful writer in the world. His works had brought enormous pleasure to millions of people who had nothing in common but that they had read Jack London, and had been thrilled by him; and they continue to sell to-day. Jack London was an adventurer, a socialist, and a writer who was born and remained one of the people. Irving Stone's biography was entitled 'Sailor on Horseback'. Others have pointed out that London was perfectly

CHAPTER 2

capable of mounting his horse and galloping off in all directions, for he was both magnificently gifted and deeply flawed. London was in love with life. He has something to tell us about leadership. He has more to tell us about the human spirit.

Origins

Jack London was born in San Francisco, California in 1876 and died in the same state 40 years later, in 1916. London was not his real father's name, but the name of the kindly, patient, civil war veteran John London with whom his mother finally settled, and whose surname Jack was glad to adopt. Jack London's real father, it seems almost certain, was an astrologer and wandering scholar called 'Professor' William Chaney, who had been in a relationship with his mother about the time that Jack was conceived. According to Stone, Chaney and Jack London were alike in both appearance and build, had similar interests, and even wrote in the same style, although their relationship was purely a genetic one and there was no environmental influence.

When contacted, Chaney denied that he was Jack's father This was devastating for Jack, who was to carry a life-long sense of insecurity for which he over-compensated with dramatic effect: for whatever Jack did, whether sailing, writing, socializing or drinking, he had to be the best—which in his book meant outdoing everyone else. Nowadays, he might be described as having an addictive personality. If he did, he made it work for him: for few have crammed so much into forty years as Jack London.

His mother was named Flora Wellman. She was a small, hard-featured, determined woman who wore spectacles and a wig. She came from a well-respected family whom she had abandoned for a life, if not quite of bohemianism, then at least of non-conformity; and she taught the piano and worked as a spiritualist. Despite her small stature and unattractive appearance, she appears to have had no trouble in attracting men. In fact, she was able to do so rather too easily. She was easily bored and ready to move on; and she did so whenever she felt the need. Her disappointments in life followed a distinct pattern. She was a strong-minded and determined woman, who was always trying something new. She started on every project with tremendous enthusiasm, but was unable to sustain her energy and commitment, so that her life became a series of failed ventures. She did, however, encourage her son to write: and for that we can be grateful.

Flora was much too preoccupied to be a proper mother to him, and Jack was mothered by his wet nurse, a former slave named Virginia Prentiss, for whom he formed a massive and enduring affection. His mother might let him down, but his former wet-nurse never did; and he even borrowed the money from her to buy his first boat. (He repaid the loan, with interest.) Jack was loyal to his real friends, and they were loyal to him. As far as his wet-nurse was concerned, Jack was colour-blind. He may have asserted the superiority of the Anglo-Saxon race in his fiction and his political views: but he did not apply that theoretical prejudice against Virginia Prentiss.

Jack London is a natural writer. His prose is simple, vivid and engaging, and his capacity for description is astonishing. His best books, such as The Call of the Wild, can easily be read in a single setting, and indeed they are impossible to put down. He showed his skill in his very first publication, about a typhoon he witnessed off the coast of Japan. London went on to overcome the many obstacles facing an unknown writer. His gifts were best suited to the short story, of which he became an acknowledged master; but he did not confine himself to that genre. In addition to his short stories and novels, he produced science fiction such as The Iron Heel, an attack on corporatism; and his book The People of the Abyss is a riveting example of investigative journalism. It is set in London in 1903, and its author had taken to the slums in the disguise of an unemployed sailor to research his subject— what it was like to live as an ordinary member of the working class at the centre of the greatest empire the world had ever known.

London was able to use his own experience to very good effect, as is shown in his account of tramping round America and begging his meals from the poor in The Road.. This is superb writing, matched only by the beginning of Martin Eden, a semi-autobiographical novel in which a young sailor wishes to get an education and make his way as a writer.

CHAPTER 2

'The one opened the door with a latch-key and went in, followed by a young fellow who awkwardly removed his cap. He wore rough clothes that smacked of the sea, and he was manifestly out of place in the spacious hall in which he found himself. He did not know what to do with his cap, and was stuffing it into his coat-pocket, when the other took it from him. The act was done quietly and naturally, and the awkward young fellow appreciated it. 'He understands,' was his thought.' He'll see me through all right.'

'He walked at the other's heels with a swing to his shoulders, and his legs spread unwittingly, as if the level floors were tilting up and sinking down to the heave and lunge of the sea. The wide rooms seemed too narrow for his rolling gait, and to himself he was in terror lest his broad shoulders should collide with the doorways or sweep the bric-a-brac from the low mantel. He recoiled from side to side between the various objects and multiplied the hazards that in reality lodged only in his mind. Between a grand piano and a centre-table piled high with books was space for a half a dozen to walk abreast, yet he essayed it with trepidation …

'An oil painting caught and held him. A heavy surf thundered and burst over an outjutting rock; lowering storm-clouds covered the sky; and, outside the line of surf, a pilot-schooner, close-hauled, heeled over till every detail of her deck was visible, was surging along against a stormy sunset sky. There was beauty, and it drew him irresistibly. He forgot his awkward walk and came closer to the painting, very close. The beauty faded out of the canvas. His face expressed his bepuzzlement. He stared at what seemed a careless daub of paint, then stepped away. Immediately all the beauty flashed back into the canvas. "A trick picture," was his thought, as he dismissed it, though in the midst of the multitudinous impressions he was receiving he found time to feel a prod of indignation that so much beauty should be sacrificed to make a trick. He did not know painting. He had been brought up on chromos and lithographs that were always definite and sharp, near or far. He had seen oil paintings, it was true, in the show windows of shops, but the glass of the windows had prevented his eager eyes from approaching too near.'

(Martin Eden, 1963, page 19.)

Jack London had an extraordinary capacity to empathize with the people of another race or era, which rose above his political prejudices and did not confine itself to recorded history. Before Adam is the dream of a civilised man who finds himself having reverted to an archaic type. The Call of the Wild is the story of Buck, a dog transplanted to Alaska, and his struggle first to survive, and then to be the leader of the pack; which is the underlying motif in much of London's writing. Both would make an excellent study of leadership: but we shall look elsewhere, to where London meets Nietszche.

The Sea Wolf

When he wrote The Sea Wolf in 1904, London was at the peak of his powers. Fascinated by philosophy, and especially by Nietzsche, he wondered what would happen if the Nietzschean Superman were brought to life—and wrote a novel to explore his idea. The German philologist and philosopher Friedrich Nietzsche (1844-1900) had rebelled against the Christianity of his forefathers—his father, grandfather and great grandfather were all Lutheran pastors—and had attacked their religion as suitable only for slaves. God, said Nietzsche, was dead; and a new morality was needed. In Beyond Good and Evil and other works, he had argued that Man should not be a submissive slave, but a dominant Superman, unfettered by conventional morality, and presumably free to be himself, without consideration for others or the common good: although he also stated that the age of the Superman would result in destruction.

What Nietzsche really meant by all this is open to question. In any event, the highly intelligent if self-taught Jack London was free to make his own interpretation; and his book about a Superman brought to life was hugely popular.

The story begins by presenting us with a narrator, a Mr Humphrey Van Weyden, who is (a little like Nietzsche himself) the opposite of the Nietzschean ideal. Humphrey Van Weyden is a man of letters,

CHAPTER 2

who has reached the age of 35 without marrying or earning his own living by the seat of his brow. He has a certain reputation in literary circles, but he has not achieved manhood. His skin is soft, his muscles are undeveloped, and his powers of exertion have never been tested.

His orderly and predictable existence is upset when his ferry is wrecked in a collision, and he is picked up from the water of Francisco Bay, half-drowned, by the sailing schooner 'Ghost', outward bound for the Sea of Japan under the command of a certain 'Wolf' Larsen.

Once he has recovered a little, Mr Van Weyden, who has a high sense of his own importance and a comfortable inheritance to cushion his existence, demands to see the captain. He has never had the experience, as an adult at any rate, of being forced to submit to someone else's will; and when he meets the captain he demands to be put ashore.[1] He will, he says, be prepared to compensate the captain for his inconvenience. Larsen, however, has other ideas. He is short-handed, and compels Van Weyden to become his cabin boy. You have never worked, he says, squeezing the other's bicep; and Van Weyden, who has hitherto rejoiced that he has others to do it for him, is forced to admit that he has not.

The captain of the sealing schooner 'Ghost' is a remarkable man. A Dane by origin, and born in the poorest of circumstances, he has raised himself entirely by his own efforts to a position where he is both owner and master of his own ship, engaged in a highly profitable trade; and there is something to admire in him, as well as much to fear or detest.

'Wolf' Larsen is not a Christian, and does not believe in the message of submission and forgiveness that is conveyed in the Sermon on the Mount. Like Nietzsche, he believes Christianity to be a slave morality, fit only for those who wish to serve rather than lead. Larsen believes in and practises the power of the will, and is prepared to accept its consequences. As he is the strongest, his will prevails. If someone else should prove stronger than him—for example, his brother, 'Death' Larsen, who has a larger, steam-powered sealing schooner and is determined to wipe his brother off the face of the earth—then Wolf Larsen does not complain of this oppression on moral grounds.

CHAPTER 2

In a world which has gone 'beyond good and evil' (the title of one of Nietzsche's works) why should anyone, including his brother as much as himself, be constrained by any form of conventional morality? Let the strong prevail!

Larsen is a man of extraordinary gifts, both physical and intellectual, and he cannot but help from exercising them. He is an experimenter in mankind, who has no concern for the adverse consequences of his actions. He adopts the effete castaway as a sort of mascot, and tries to make a man out of him. It is an experience that his unfortunate 'cabin-boy' would have given a great deal to avoid.

In Chapter Eleven, Larsen exercises his power over his new crewman.

> 'You are afraid of me. You cannot deny it. If I should catch you by the throat, thus,"—his hand was about my throat and my breath was shut off,—"and began to press the life out of you thus, and thus, your instinct of immortality will go glimmering, and your instinct of life, which is longing for life, will flutter up, and you will struggle to save yourself. Eh? I see the fear of death in your eyes. You beat the air with your arms. You exert all your puny strength to struggle to live. Your hand is clutching my arm, lightly it feels as a butterfly resting there. Your chest is heaving, your tongue protruding, your skin turning dark, your eyes swimming. 'To live! To live! To live!' you are crying; and you are crying to live here and now, not hereafter. You doubt your immortality, eh? Ha! ha! You are not sure of it. You won't chance it. This life only you are certain is real. Ah, it is growing dark and darker. It is the darkness of death, the ceasing to be, the ceasing to feel, the ceasing to move, that is gathering about you, descending upon you, rising around you. Your eyes are becoming set. They are glazing. My voice sounds faint and far. You cannot see my face. And still you struggle in my grip. You kick with your legs. Your body draws itself up in knots like a snake's. Your chest heaves and strains. To live! To live! To live—"

CHAPTER 2

> I heard no more. Consciousness was blotted out by the darkness he had so graphically described, and when I came to myself I was lying on the floor and he was smoking a cigar and regarding me thoughtfully with that old familiar light of curiosity in his eyes.
>
> "Well, have I convinced you?" he demanded. "Here take a drink of this. I want to ask you some questions."
>
> I rolled my head negatively on the floor. "Your arguments are too—er—forcible," I managed to articulate, at cost of great pain to my aching throat.
>
> "You'll be all right in half-an-hour," he assured me. "And I promise I won't use any more physical demonstrations. Get up now. You can sit on a chair.'"

In Chapter Twelve, the situation on board worsens, as Larsen provokes rebellion, and demonstrates that he is prepared to brutalize any man for any offence, especially those who have shown any independence of spirit.

> 'The last twenty-four hours have witnessed a carnival of brutality. From cabin to forecastle it seems to have broken out like a contagion. I scarcely know where to begin. Wolf Larsen was really the cause of it. The relations among the men, strained and made tense by feuds, quarrels and grudges, were in a state of unstable equilibrium, and evil passions flared up in flame like prairie-grass.
>
> [A seaman] Johnson, it seems, bought a suit of oilskins from the slop-chest and found them to be of greatly inferior quality... But of Johnson's grumbling at the slop-chest I knew nothing, so that what I witnessed came with a shock of sudden surprise. I had just finished sweeping the cabin, and had been inveigled by Wolf Larsen into a discussion of Hamlet, his favourite Shakespearian character, when Johansen (the ship's mate) descended the companion stairs followed by Johnson. The latter's cap came off after the custom of the sea, and he stood respectfully in the centre of the cabin, swaying heavily and uneasily to the roll of the schooner and facing the captain.

CHAPTER 2

"Shut the doors and draw the slide," Wolf Larsen said to me.

As I obeyed I noticed an anxious light come into Johnson's eyes, but I did not dream of its cause. I did not dream of what was to occur until it did occur, but he knew from the very first what was coming and awaited it bravely. And in his action I found complete refutation of all Wolf Larsen's materialism. The sailor Johnson was swayed by idea, by principle, and truth, and sincerity. He was right, he knew he was right, and he was unafraid. He would die for the right if needs be, he would be true to himself, sincere with his soul. And in this was portrayed the victory of the spirit over the flesh, the indomitability and moral grandeur of the soul that knows no restriction and rises above time and space and matter with a surety and invincibleness born of nothing else than eternity and immortality.'

"'Look at him, Hump," Wolf Larsen said to me, "look at this bit of animated dust, this aggregation of matter that moves and breathes and defies me and thoroughly believes itself to be compounded of something good; that is impressed with certain human fictions such as righteousness and honesty, and that will live up to them in spite of all personal discomforts and menaces. What do you think of him, Hump? What do you think of him?"

"I think that he is a better man than you are," I answered, impelled, somehow, with a desire to draw upon myself a portion of the wrath I felt was about to break upon his head. "His human fictions, as you choose to call them, make for nobility and manhood. You have no fictions, no dreams, no ideals. You are a pauper."

He nodded his head with a savage pleasantness. "Quite true, Hump, quite true. I have no fictions that make for nobility and manhood. A living dog is better than a dead lion, say I with the Preacher. My only doctrine is the doctrine of expediency, and it makes for surviving. This bit of the ferment we call 'Johnson,' when he is no longer a bit of the ferment, only dust and ashes, will have no more nobility than any dust and ashes, while I shall still be alive and roaring."

CHAPTER 2

"Do you know what I am going to do?" he questioned.

I shook my head.

"Well, I am going to exercise my prerogative of roaring and show you how fares nobility. Watch me."

Three yards away from Johnson he was, and sitting down. Nine feet! And yet he left the chair in full leap, without first gaining a standing position. He left the chair, just as he sat in it, squarely, springing from the sitting posture like a wild animal, a tiger, and like a tiger covered the intervening space. It was an avalanche of fury that Johnson strove vainly to fend off. .... I cannot give the further particulars of the horrible scene that followed. ... It was too much for me to witness. I felt that I should lose my mind, and I ran up the companion stairs to open the doors and escape on deck. But Wolf Larsen, leaving his victim for the moment, and with one of his tremendous springs, gained my side and flung me into the far corner of the cabin.

"The phenomena of life, Hump," he girded at me. "Stay and watch it. You may gather data on the immortality of the soul. Besides, you know, we can't hurt Johnson's soul. It's only the fleeting form we may demolish."

It seemed centuries—possibly it was no more than ten minutes that the beating continued. ...

"Jerk open the doors,—Hump," I was commanded.

I obeyed, and the two brutes picked up the senseless man like a sack of rubbish and hove him clear up the companion stairs, through the narrow doorway, and out on deck. The blood from his nose gushed in a scarlet stream over the feet of the helmsman, who was none other than Louis, his boat-mate. But Louis took and gave a spoke and gazed imperturbably into the binnacle.[2]

Not so was the conduct of George Leach, the erstwhile cabin-boy. Fore and aft there was nothing that could have surprised us more than his consequent behaviour. He it was that came up on the poop without orders and dragged Johnson forward, where he set about dressing his wounds as well as he could and making him comfortable. Johnson, as Johnson, was unrecognizable ...

"May God damn your soul to hell, Wolf Larsen, only hell's too good for you, you coward, you murderer, you pig!" was his opening salutation.

I was thunderstruck. I looked for his instant annihilation. But it was not Wolf Larsen's whim to annihilate him. He sauntered slowly forward to the break of the poop, and, leaning his elbow on the corner of the cabin, gazed down thoughtfully and curiously at the excited boy.'

Larsen soon revenges himself on the rebellious Leach, and both he and Johnson meet a watery death. The Ghost continues on her brutal course until there is an outright mutiny, which Larsen quells by sheer force. The hitherto effete Van Weyden, meanwhile, is beginning to acquire both some muscle and some understanding of what life in Larsen's world is really about, and has been promoted from cabin boy to first officer as a further experiment by his unusual captain.

In the end, Larsen is defeated, and has no grounds for complaint. Firstly, the 'Ghost' rather improbably rescues another literary castaway, a cultivated young woman named Maud Brewster who is already an admirer of Humphrey Van Weyden's prose. Maud Brewster provides a new form of challenge to Captain Larsen's authority, for she is not afraid of him, and she represents something that he cannot crush. Secondly, he is betrayed by his body itself. Larsen has begun to suffer from blinding headaches, during which he retires to his cabin and a state of near unconsciousness. As he is about to ravish Maud, his body finally rejects his will, and his power is at an end.

Humphrey Van Weyden has survived his ordeal. Larsen is dying, and no longer a potent force, and he has the ship, the woman and the future at his feet. He has learned to stand up for himself, and to be a man. He has learned to cope with adversity, and to exercise a version of leadership in the most trying of circumstances; and he has retained some sort of dignity and self-respect. We might even claim that he has

CHAPTER 2

demonstrated the flaws in his captain's philosophy of materialism. So he may have done; but he is not the person, I would suggest, whom we remember from this novel. That person is Wolf Larsen.

Commentary

The Sea Wolf is a fascinating story, if a little one-sided: for the only really interesting person is Wolf Larsen himself. The remainder of the crew of the Ghost are sketched in very lightly, and we never meet Wolf's nemesis, his brother 'Death' Larsen, the master of the steam-driven sealing ship Macedonia. We feel some sympathy for Johnson, the honourable and courageous seaman who stands up for human dignity against his captain; but his campaign is very short-lived, for both he and his supporter Leach meet an early fate.

As for Humphrey Van Weyden, the ostensible hero of the book, and the weakling who finally discovers his manhood—his weaknesses are so very strongly delineated at the beginning of the story that it is difficult if not impossible to feel overmuch sympathy for him. This is in part a problem of style, which changes as the story progresses. Humphrey Van Weyden and Maud Brewster create between them a sort of literary salon in the saloon of the Ghost. In their chaste and bloodless sea-board romance, Van Weyden's only rival is the hitherto entirely dominant master of the vessel. So lifeless are the two lovers of literature, and so deeply lacking in authenticity is their relationship, that one feels almost sympathetic to the Superman as he decides to take Miss Brewster by force. He is prevented from so doing neither by her feeble resistance nor his unlikely first officer's futile intervention, but by the worsening of mysterious and incapacitating illness; and we therefore lose the possibility of a rather more interesting story.

D H Lawrence might have made Maud Brewster fall for the Superman as the first real force in her life, and Hollywood would, no doubt, have had Beauty tame the Beast[3]; but London does not choose either path, and we are left with an unsatisfactory ending, more appropriate to a sentimental novelette, in which Larsen finally dies of his mysterious illness and the two lovers, still chaste, are rescued by a passing steamer and thereby 'saved from themselves', in the final words of the book.

Why did London construct his novel in this way, and what is he trying to tell us? We may be mistaken in searching for a coherence that is not in the text. London was a better short story writer than a novelist, and was not always master of his plot. Moreover, he was always under pressure. He had to write furiously in order to earn enough money to provide for both his dependants and his interests; and he may simply have chosen to finish off his Superman, and move on to his next challenge.

South of the Slot

London was capable of a better ending, and we see it elsewhere in his work. In his short story, South of the Slot, Freddie Drummond leads a double life as an academic sociologist who distances himself from real emotions and a trade union leader (known as 'Big' Bill Totts) who actively engages in the struggle. Naturally, the two men are attracted to very different women. Bill Totts has fallen, hook, line and sinker, for Mary Condon, a labour agitator and strike leader who leaps from the page as 'a royal-bodied woman, graceful and sinewy as a panther, with amazing black eyes...'

Realizing the danger she presents to his other self, Freddie Drummond sets out to woo (in a chaste and bloodless way) Catherine Van Vorst, an academic and the daughter of an academic, who is cold, reserved, aristocratic and 'wholesomely conservative.' She is the right woman to save him from the panther, he thinks; but he needs to pay one more call south of the slot, in order to complete his research...

> 'So Freddie Drummond went down for the last time as Bill Totts, got his data, and, unfortunately, encountered Mary Condon. Once more installed in his study, it was not a pleasant thing to look back upon. It made his warning doubly imperative. Bill Totts had behaved abominably. Not only had he met Mary Condon at the Central Labor Council, but he had stopped in at a chop-house with her, on the way home, and treated her to oysters. And before they parted at her door, his arms had been about her, and he had kissed her on the lips and kissed her repeatedly. And her last words in his ear, words uttered softly

with a catchy sob in the throat that was nothing more nor less than a love cry, were "Bill . . . dear, dear Bill."

Freddie Drummond shuddered at the recollection. He saw the pit yawning for him. He was not by nature a polygamist, and he was appalled at the possibilities of the situation. It would have to be put an end to, and it would end in one only of two ways: either he must become wholly Bill Totts and be married to Mary Condon, or he must remain wholly Freddie Drummond and be married to Catherine Van Vorst. Otherwise, his conduct would be beneath contempt and horrible.'

In the end, (of course), the activist triumphs in the contest for the disputed soul of this highly convincing fictional creation.

Compare also London's superbly written semi-autobiographical novel Martin Eden, in which the eponymous hero, a sailor who wishes to educate himself and become a writer, falls for a cultivated young woman, the pale and ethereal Ruth: only to realize that her education is a sham, that she is afraid of life, and that she is unable to think for herself. He does not remain with her; and he does not need to be 'saved from himself.'

Lessons on leadership

London's ending for The Sea Wolf is flawed. But he had, as Ambrose Bierce wrote, succeeded in the creation of Wolf Larsen, which was a major achievement for any novelist. What does the book tell us about leadership? There is a minor lesson here for leaders, as for everyone, that it is as well to learn to stand on one's own two feet; and Larsen's behaviour to Humphrey Van Weyden helps him to develop both in physique and character, whatever the motives of his developer. But it is the Sea Wolf himself who absorbs our interest. London has succeeded in his ambition of creating a character who is by any conventional standard thoroughly immoral, and whose exploitation of his own strength should excite both our horror and condemnation; but who never ceases to fascinate.

Larsen's appeal, if that is the right word, is not the simple fascination of evil. Any competent writer should be able to create a convincing villain; and any villain will attract our attention because he appeals to the suppressed side of our own personality. But Larsen is unusual in that he is neither stage villain nor mindless psychopath. Nor does he become the tearful repentant and seeker of sympathy into whom a lesser novelist, with a different purpose, might have transformed him. He is true to the ideals that he does not have, and does not expect that pity from others that he would not have given them; and as his magnificent body turns against him and his strength, like that of Samson, departs, his questing mind remains active to the end.

Is his death a punishment for the wicked, meted out by a moralistic author? Is he, perhaps, facing the consequences of sexual misadventure, to which London could only hint under the literary constraints of the 1900s? We think not. Larsen's fate is the corollary of his materialist view of the world. He is the Superman, until a stronger version comes along, or the machine on which he depends breaks down of its own accord; and although London strives not to say so, there is something almost robotic, and certainly inhuman, in his strength. The terminator triumphs, until he himself is terminated; and there are no rights and wrongs in such a contest, for it is indeed beyond good and evil.

Questions for reflection

- In *The Sea Wolf*, Jack London attempts to bring Nietzsche's philosophy to life, and to create a convincing portrayal of a superman. Does he succeed?

- What do you make of Wolf Larsen's behaviour, from an ethical point of view? Is he entitled to act as he chooses? Why does he not appear to feel shame, guilt or remorse when he acts in such a way as to offend against any generally recognized moral code?

CHAPTER 2

- Larsen's main adversary in the book is Humphrey van Weyden, a feeble parasite (in Larsen's view) who nevertheless finds the strength to stand up to his tormentor. What does 'Hump' learn from his voyage on the *Ghost*?

- Whose attitude to life do you prefer: that of Wolf Larsen or Humphrey van Weyden?

Commentary on questions

- In *The Sea Wolf*, Jack London attempts to bring Nietzsche's philosophy to life, and to create a convincing portrayal of a superman. Does he succeed?

In our view, yes: London succeeds in his creation. Whether or not Nietszche would agree with that judgement is beyond our ken.

- What do you make of Wolf Larsen's behaviour, from an ethical point of view? Is he entitled to act as he chooses? Why does he not appear to feel shame, guilt or remorse when he acts in such a way as to offend against any generally recognized moral code?

Whether or not Larsen's behaviour can be described as ethical depends upon whether or not one accepts Nietszche's philosophy as a basis for behaviour. Larsen is both consistent and coherent in his actions and his justification for them, and therefore could be said to be acting ethically, i.e. in accord with his espoused principles. As it happens, we disagree with Nietszche's views, whether as a basis for morality or social life—which may come to the same thing. Man is a social animal, and social life would be impossible without some element of compromise and reciprocity.

- Larsen's main adversary in the book is Humphrey van Weyden, a feeble parasite (in Larsen's view) who nevertheless finds the strength to stand up to his tormentor. What does 'Hump' learn from his voyage on the *Ghost*?

CHAPTER 2

The voyage of the Ghost is a rite de passage in more senses than one, and 'Hump' learns a great deal from it. His fundamental convictions are challenged, and he learns to articulate and stand up for them. He learns courage, self-reliance, and assertiveness; and he learns to fight for and win Maud Brewster. If we were to take a Marxian perspective, we might say that 'Hump' learns from the experience of working with his hands and acquiring practical skills, since his previous experience of life has been purely that of an intellectual who benefited unfairly from the division of labour which enabled him to live a life of luxury at others' expense, and stopped him from realising his potential. In the future communist society of which Marx dreamed, there would be no division of labour.

> ☐ Whose attitude to life do you prefer: that of Wolf Larsen or Humphrey van Weyden?

A personal preference, in which I should have to vote for Larsen, despite his brutality. There remains something of the goody-goody about van Weyden, and I never warm to him. I began this chapter by saying that London was an outstanding short story writer. I conclude it by recommending once again to readers his tale South of the Slot, in which Freddie Drummond becomes Big Bill Totts, and embraces, not the brutal side of his nature, but the joy of life itself.

Notes

1. Harvey Cheyne, Junior, undergoes a comparable experience in Rudyard Kipling's Captains Courageous, which was explored in Chapter One. In this case, the young and spoiled heir to an immense fortune falls off a liner, and is rescued by a doryman and taken aboard the We're Here!, a cod-fishing vessel heading for the Grand Banks. Her master, Disko Troop, refuses to believe that Cheyne could possibly afford to pay for his vessel to be turned around, and makes him a member of the crew. However, Disko Troop and Wolf Larsen are very different masters, and the apprenticeship which they force on their new crew members is a very different experience.
2. Louis, in other words, was steering. A ship's wheel has spokes and the ship's compass is contained in a binnacle. London, an enthusiastic sailor, assumes this as common knowledge.

CHAPTER 2

3   Larsen was played by Edward G Robinson in one of several Hollywood versions of The Sea Wolf; the Superman as snarl. Captains Courageous fared better: Spenser Tracy made an acceptable Portuguese doryman. All of the authors mentioned in this book have had some of their works adapted for the screen, and all of those screen adaptations, good, bad, but rarely indifferent, have made their impact upon popular conceptions of leadership.

CHAPTER 3

For Whom the Bell Tolls: Ernest Hemingway

No man is an Iland, intire of it selfe; every man is a peece of the Continente, a part of the maine; if a Clod bee washed away by the Sea, Europe is the lesse, as well as if a Promontorie were, as well as if a Mannor of thy friends or of thine own were; any mans death diminishes me, because I am involved in Mankind; And therefore never send to know for whom the bell tolls; It tolls for thee.

John Donne

Ernest Hemingway, the great American writer, has had a remarkable influence upon the politicians who have grown up whilst reading his books—possibly, indeed, they may have grown up, to some extent, through reading his books—and the New York Times commented that Hemingway had been essential reading for both candidates in the 2008 electoral contest for the presidency of the United States.

According to David Margolick, few figures, real or imaginary, exerted as much influence on Senator John McCain as Robert Jordan, the fictional American volunteering for the Republican side in the Spanish Civil War. McCain, in fact, borrowed the title for his 2002 autobiography Worth the Fighting For from words delivered by Robert Jordan, the main character in Hemingway's novel For Whom the Bell Tolls, first published in 1940.

McCain, who first discovered the Hemingway novel when he was twelve years old, told another journalist, Jon Meacham, that "Robert Jordan is what I always thought a man ought to be." In Jordan, McCain writes, he discovered someone who was "brave, dedicated, capable, selfless," a man who "possessed in abundance that essence of courage that Hemingway described as grace under pressure, a man who would risk his life but never his honour." Expressing what McCain calls "beautiful fatalism," Jordan is "an individual committed to a cause he believes in."

In life, to use McCain's words from a 2002 interview, "There may be events you can't control but as long as you remain true to your ideals, your beliefs and your causes, then it is okay and you're willing to accept your fate." Jordan not only inspired McCain but seemed real to him. As a prisoner of war in Hanoi, McCain thought if Jordan were in the cell next to his, Hemingway's hero "would be stoic, he would be strong, he would be tough, he wouldn't give up. And Robert would expect me to do the same thing."

Margolick also notes that "Senator Barack Obama told Rolling Stone that Hemingway's novel is one of the three books that most inspired him." As we all know, Senator Barack Obama won the election: which left the former war hero John McCain free to display that grace under pressure which he had so admired in Hemingway's fiction.

Who was Ernest Hemingway, what did he convey about leadership in his fiction, and why has he been so influential?

Life

Ernest Hemingway was born in 1899 in a suburb of Chicago, Illinois, the son of a successful doctor and his musical wife. Although popular and successful in all school activities, he was restless, and left school at sixteen to become a journalist. This decision was to influence his style thereafter as a novelist—a subject to which we shall return.

Like Rudyard Kipling, who also began his writing career as a journalist, Ernest Hemingway was short-sighted. However, that did not stop him from leading an active life. Hemingway was a keen sportsman who boxed, wrestled, and swam at school, and continued to practise sports into middle age: he also rode, shot big game, skied, climbed mountains and fished for shark. He was fascinated by bull-fighting, and one of his most popular books, The Sun Also Rises, is devoted to that passion.

Hemingway was clearly determined to prove himself, in one way or another: and in 1918 he left his work as a journalist in America and became a Red Cross ambulance-driver for the Italian army, serving against the Austro-Hungarian Empire on the Eastern Front. Hemingway was severely wounded by shrapnel, and spent some time in a military hospital. By the time he was discharged, the war was over: and he was to write a novel about his experience, A Farewell to Arms, which was widely praised.

Ernest Hemingway was determined to be a writer of fiction, although he also continued to work as a journalist. He made his way to Paris, the natural home of all writers, artists, poets and other Bohemians in the 1920s. France was cheap, especially if one could take advantage of the exchange rate; and the cost of living in Paris was very low. It was full of artists; it was a centre of intellectual ferment; and it was exciting.[1] Here Hemingway married his first of four wives, and began to write his novels and short stories in the cafes where the artistic set gathered, at the same time taking trips to southern France and Spain to ski, to mountaineer, and to pursue his passion for the bull-fight. Hemingway was the opposite of a dilettante artist, and despite his image as a man of action, devoted to the occupation of writing. He was disciplined, he worked hard, and he was productive.

The Spanish Civil War: Nationalists v. Republicans

The Spanish Civil War began in 1936[2], when a group of army generals, led by Francisco Franco, staged a coup against the elected government, which they saw as having betrayed Spain. (They were known as the Nationalists.) Their coup was only partially successful, and Madrid and Barcelona remained in Republican hands. Both sides set out to gather international support, without which neither could succeed. The Nationalists obtained support from Fascist Italy and Nazi Germany. The Republicans obtained the backing of Communist Russia[3], as well as the general support of left-wing international opinion. (The United Kingdom and France remained neutral, pursuing a policy of non-intervention which was intended to prevent the war from becoming an interntational conflict, but which left Germany and Italy free to

CHAPTER 3

act as they chose.) Opinion was put into practice by the International Brigades, young men and women who volunteered to fight or nurse in Spain in support of the Republican cause. Many of them were to sacrifice their lives for their ideals in a war which ended in 1939 with Franco triumphant.

Hemingway, the writer who saw himself as a man of action, was fascinated by war, sympathetic to the Republican cause, and liked to be at the heart of the action. He was by now a famous and highly influential writer, living mainly in America. In 1937 he travelled to Spain with another journalist, Martha Gelhorn, and became a war correspondent. At the same time, he began to gather his impressions for his next novel. In 1940 he married Martha and published his outstanding novel of the Spanish civil war, For Whom the Bell Tolls.

During the Second World War, 'Papa' Hemingway worked as a war correspondent, and as usual managed to find his way into the thick of the action, being present at the liberation of Paris. After the war, his life of heavy drinking and damaging accidents began to take its toll. Hemingway spent less time in 'macho' activities, although he continued to fish for shark. By now a world-famous and immensely successful writer, he was able to afford to live where he chose; and he spent much of his time on his ranch in Cuba, where he did not approve of the regime in power[4], but continued to write, eventually winning the Nobel Prize for Literature for his late, great book The Old Man and the Sea.

Hemingway suffered increasingly poor health and finally decided that he had no wish to lead the life of an invalid. At the age of sixty, he shot himself at his home in Idaho. In committing suicide Hemingway was following the example of his father, who had been depressed for much of his life; and his brother, sister and grand-daughter were also to kill themselves. He was also following the example of the American writer Jack London, who had found it impossible to continue to live as he wished. Both men were able to fit a huge amount into their lives; both had a major impact; and both left a literary legacy which can easily be exploited for ideas on leadership.

Hemingway, the Nobel Prize winner, was the more accomplished novelist. He created clear plots with believable characters and his books address enduring themes. He is, however, perhaps most admired for his style. This may seem a little surprising, in that Hemingway's books are written with such apparent ease as to seem almost without a style. However, that is the result of his craftsmanship as a writer and is not an accident. Very few artists create a work of art without labouring over it, however artless the final product may appear: and Hemingway was a consummate artist.

Style: *The Killers*

Hemingway was a great and original writer and his style has been much imitated (and indeed parodied) but never surpassed. His aim was to use as few words as possible to convey the sensation and effect that he wanted, and at times his prose reads almost like the journalism that was his first training. His sentences are short and contain very few adjectives, and he tells his story as simply as possible, with good use of dialogue and almost no descriptive passages. He is excellent at conveying atmosphere. In his first published short story, The Killers, an old boxer and former criminal, Ole Andreson, lies on his bed in a rented room, waiting for the killers who intend to bring his life to an abrupt end. He is warned of what is about to happen by a young man, Nick Adams, who works in the local diner; but Ole chooses to accept his destiny. He is tired of running and he has nowhere to go. Let them come.

Hemingway conveys his mood, and the hopelessness of his position, with a very few words. It is a sketch rather than a full picture, but a sketch that enables the reader to fill in the details and to imagine the full story for himself. The story begins at the diner at five o'clock, as the two killers Max and Al, arrive to prepare their ambush. We learn how they are dressed, in overcoats that are too tight for them. We learn what they would have liked to eat: for they appear to be either too stupid or too arrogant to understand that they cannot have the evening menu until six o'clock. We learn that Max is the bully and

CHAPTER 3

the loudmouth of the two, and that both men have to impress their audience as tough guys. And we learn why they are there. But let us see how Hemingway starts the story.

'The door of Henry's lunch-room opened and two men came in. They sat down at the counter. 'What's yours?' George asked them.

'I don't know,' one of the men said. 'What do you want to eat, Al?' 'I don't know,' said Al. 'I don't know what I want to eat.'

Outside it was getting dark. The street light came on outside the window. The two men at the counter read the menu. From the other end of the counter Nick Adams watched them...

'Give me bacon and eggs,' said the other man. He was about the same size as Al. Their faces were different, but they were dressed like twins. Both wore overcoats too tight for them. They sat leaning forward, their elbows on the counter ...

George put down two platters, one of ham and eggs, the other of bacon and eggs, on the counter. He set down two side dishes of fried potatoes and closed the wicket into the kitchen.

'Which is yours?' he asked Al.

'Don't you remember?'

'Ham and eggs.'

'Just a bright boy,' Max said. He leaned forward and took the ham and eggs. Both men ate with their gloves on. George watched them eat.

'What are you looking at?' Max looked at George.

'Nothing.'

'The hell you were. You were looking at me.'

'Maybe the boy meant it for a joke, Max,' Al said.

George laughed.

'You don't have to laugh,' Max said to him. 'You don't have to laugh at all, see?'

CHAPTER 3

Hemingway is a master in the art of dramatic irony and in the systematic creation of tension. We understand what is going on, and why Al and Max are a threat, because of the atmosphere he creates. The detail is both necessary and absorbing, and builds up a picture in our minds: a young man, Nick, who serves in a diner; his friend George, who is less inclined to become involved in what happens; Sam, the black cook in the kitchen, whose only significant utterance is the most memorable comment in the whole text; and the two small, fastidiously-dressed gangsters, Al and Max, who come in and examine the menu, but are really there for quite another purpose.

In another writer's hands, the detail would seem excessive, and perhaps pedestrian: but not with Hemingway. His story builds towards an outcome is all the more impressive for not being made explicit. We are there. We share the thoughts of Nick; of the other men in the room; and of the old boxer, Ole Andreson, whom the two gunmen have come to kill, and who is tired of running. We anticipate his fate, and we realise that he cannot avoid it. It is in how others react to the killers and the moral dilemma that they pose, by which we can assess their characters. Nick wants to do something, but George does not. The cook, Sam, is sardonic about Nick's self-confidence:

"Little boys always know what to do."

As a black man, he knows that Max and Al would kill him as easily as swatting a fly, and he has a right to protect himself. Ole Andreson himself is fatalistic, as we have already seen. Or perhaps he is just tired. Mrs Bell, who helps his landlady, does not really understand what is happening, but is attracted to the Swede. Again, this is an impression that Hemingway conveys with a single remark, and leaves the rest of the work to us. This is a strong story, with a strong line. It is Hemingway at his taut best.

Personality

Was Ernest Hemingway the macho he-man that he seems to have wanted to be, and are his works, almost in their entirety, a homage to masculinity? Was he a sort of second Jack London, who had made

CHAPTER 3

his reputation writing about the search for gold in the Klondyke, when men were men and women charged for their services—or did not appear at all? That would be a gross caricature of both writers. Like Jack London, Hemingway was fascinated by travel, boxing and war; and there is a certain similarity not only in their writing but in their habits. Both drank heavily—one of London's strongest works, John Barleycorn, is sub-titled Alcoholic Memoirs—and both were womanisers. In some ways, Hemingway was the more accomplished writer: for London was never really able to move from the short story, of which he was admittedly a master, to the novel.

Hemingway wrote about masculine habits and values, but his work is more than superior pulp fiction. Hemingway defined courage as grace under pressure; and his fiction explores that grace. Hemingway may have wished to be a man of action, but he was primarily a writer. It was his task to convey to his readers the experiences that they might never have, but which they could share through his fiction. Let us see how he does so in perhaps his most acclaimed novel.

For whom the bell tolls

Robert Jordan, a self-reliant and highly competent young American idealist, is working for the republicans as an explosives expert during the Spanish civil war (1936-1939). As the story begins he has climbed high in the mountains in fascist-occupied central Spain to play his part in a major set-piece attack by the republicans against the fascists. The republican forces, commanded by the Russian Comrade General Golz, are to mount a surprise attack on a defended fascist position. Once the attack has begun, it is predictable that the fascists will rush reinforcements to the attacked area, by a certain route. That route must cross a certain bridge, high in the mountains, where Robert Jordan will be waiting with his trusty dynamite and his somewhat less trustworthy guerrilla comrades. After the republican offensive has commenced, Jordan will attack and destroy the bridge. Fascist reinforcements will not arrive; the fascist defence will fail; Golz's divisional attack will succeed; and the republicans will win a province.

That, at any rate, is the plan. As all military strategists know, no plan survives contact with the enemy; and this plan has fundamental flaws even before the enemy is encountered. General Golz has no confidence that the forces of which he is officially in command, who are in reality a loose coalition rather than a trained professional army, will be able to mount a co-ordinated attack at the agreed time; and he has even less confidence, if that were possible, that the plan will remain a secret. Once the fascists know what is coming, they will be able to thwart his stratagems; and they will increase the guard on an already defended bridge.

Robert Jordan, meanwhile, has reconnoitred the bridge and is confident that he can destroy it. However, he does not have the same confidence in his new allies. Anselmo, who has guided him into the mountains, is reliable: but Anselmo, although extremely fit, is 68 years old. The guerrilla band whose help he will need to capture the bridge is led by Pablo: and Pablo does not seem a man he can trust. Firstly, he is hostile to the newcomer: and secondly, there is the sadness of defeat about him. Here is how Hemingway describes the situation, though Jordan's eyes.

> 'You had to trust people completely or not at all, and you had to make decisions about the trusting... Robert Jordan trusted the old man, Anselmo, so far in everything except judgement. He had not yet had an opportunity to trust his judgement...' (page 6)

As for Pablo, however, he did not inspire confidence. In the first place, he was an ugly, unprepossessing man.

> 'Robert Jordan looked at the man's heavy, beard-stubbled face. It was almost round and his head was round and set close on his shoulders. His eyes were small and set too wide apart...' (pages 11, 12)

More important than his appearance, however, was his demeanour.

> 'In his sullenness there was a sadness that was disturbing to Robert Jordan. He knew that sadness and to see it here worried him. I don't like that sadness, he thought. That sadness is bad.

CHAPTER 3

That's the sadness they get before they quit or betray...' (pages 14, 15)

As if that were not enough, Pablo is pessimistic and has clearly had enough of being chased. He has seen the fascists become stronger, and no longer believes his side will win. Now, he simply wants to survive.

> "*They* are very strong," Pablo said. It was as though he were talking to himself. He looked at the horses gloomily. "You do not realize how strong they are. I see them always stronger, always better armed. Always with more material. Here am I with horses like these. And what can I look forward to? To be hunted and to die. Nothing more."' (page 17)

Moreover, Pablo resents Jordan's arrival as a threat to his authority and to the safety of the group.

> "'I am tired of being hunted... I am tired of all this. You hear?" He turned to Robert Jordan. "What right have you, a foreigner, to come here and tell me what I must do?"' (page 17)

Jordan assesses Pablo as a high risk.

> 'They (the Spanish guerrillas) are wonderful when they are good, he (Jordan) thought. There is no people like them when they are good and when they go bad there is no people that is worse.... You... know (Pablo) is going bad fast and without hiding it. When he starts to hide it he will have made a decision. Remember that, he told himself. The first friendly thing he does, he will have made a decision.' (page 19)

Jordan's assessment proves correct. When Pablo does turn friendly, it is because he has made a decision; and that decision is to betray the cause.

Up to that point, Jordan faces a major problem in deciding what to do. Pablo is an unreliable and potentially treacherous leader who should be replaced before the republican offensive begins and it is too late to do so. However, Jordan has no authority to replace him, and it would be highly risky for him to take sides in a domestic issue. If he does intervene, through force of circumstances, he cannot be sure that his intervention will be accepted. It is highly likely that Pablo's guerrilla gang will turn on him as a foreigner, even if he does speak Spanish. Pablo is their man, and has fought bravely in the past, even if he is now a drunkard and a pessimist. Moreover, his pessimism about Golz's set-piece attack is justified—although that is not something that Jordan would wish to admit to the group as a whole, for morale must be maintained.

The Spanish republicans are intensely nationalistic, even in the middle of a civil war. They admire the fascists who show courage, even as they slit their throats; and they have no fundamental loyalty to Jordan, the Ingles. He can only win them over by patriotic appeal, which is unlikely, coming from him, to win many arguments; by force of personality; and by the surgical use of violence as a last resort.

Like a bull-fighter, Jordan is on the horns of a dilemma. Should he kill Pablo? If so, when? Timing is everything: and he can only act when he senses that the mood of the group is with him. He says to himself, after one such missed opportunity:

> 'I am tired, he thought, and perhaps my judgment is not good... If it is true, as the gypsy says, that they expected me to kill Pablo then I should have done that. But it was never clear that they did expect that. For a stranger to kill where he must work with the people afterwards is very bad.' (page 66)

As it happens, he delays any such decision for too long, and Pablo is left alive to damage the cause—even though Jordan has his pistol cocked and ready to shoot him on more than one occasion. We must acknowledge, however, that if he fails to kill Pablo, Jordan is able to engineer a situation in which Pilar takes command of the group; and she is a courageous and determined leader.

Jordan's qualities

In his quandary, Jordan is too hesitant to act; but in another sense he is already showing the grace under pressure that is Hemingway's definition of courage. Jordan is a realistic idealist. He accepts the position as it is, and does not waste time wishing that things were otherwise. He might have paraded his resentment at the way he was being treated by Pablo. He might have pointed out that he was there as a volunteer, risking his life and limb for a cause which was not his own, and that he deserved co-operation and support: but Jordan knows that such a declaration would have been disastrous. The high sierra is no place for self-righteous pride.

He must work with these people and not against them; and for a foreign explosives expert working with a Spanish guerrilla band, the band is almost always right, and he is almost always wrong. If he wants to avoid unnecessary trouble, he should not approach any of their women; and he should never suggest that there is a better way of doing things. (Being human, Jordan does both. He regrets losing his self-control in suggesting another way of doing things: but he does not regret falling in love with Maria.)

As he reflects later in the story:

> 'Of course they turned on you [i.e. Jordan himself]. They turned on you often but they always turned on everyone. They turned on themselves, too.' (page 142)

Love in the high sierra

In the three days of the time-span of this intense story, much happens. Jordan, the ascetic young man who has no time for women, falls in love with Maria, the damaged but beautiful young partisan who has been beaten and raped by Moorish soldiers; they make love, and decide to marry when they can. Pablo proves a wily opponent who shows political skills and knows how to survive by apparent concession. He allows his woman, Pilar, an older revolutionary, to take command of the group (as well as remaining as its cook, assisted by Maria) and bides his time until he can destroy Jordan. Pilar, meanwhile, is the joker in the pack.

The importance of being Pilar

Jordan comes to terms with Pilar, who is a woman of both passion and judgement and proves a worthy leader of the band. In some ways she proves a better leader than Jordan would have been, for although she may not have his knowledge of explosives or understanding of military strategy, she is better at working with people, and she has the ultimate advantage of being Spanish. Pilar is old, at least by her own account (she is 48.) She is large, ugly, masculine in appearance and with a deep voice, and has had many lovers: she has a penchant for bull-fighters, even if they are unsuccessful in the ring, and she lives life to extremes.

Nevertheless, she has a sense of humour, if a scouring tongue: and she is a more rounded person than Jordan, who although he tells himself jokes is rather too serious for his new colleagues, and has not reached Pilar's level of understanding of human nature. Pilar, however, is in poor health, for the excesses of her previous life have caught up with her; and although she has a strong personality in her own right, and is respected for herself, there is a limit to what she can achieve in so masculine a society.

El Sordo and his demise

Jordan makes contact with El Sordo, the leader of another guerrilla gang in the mountains who would have proved a much more worthy supporter than Pablo; but El Sordo and his followers are wiped out in a fascist attack which combines mounted infantry and air-power. Jordan discovers that another of his supporters, the gypsy Rafael, seems wholly unreliable: he leaves his sentry post near the cave in order to kill two rabbits for the pot, and as a result a fascist cavalry patrol nearly finds and kills them all. But it is with men like Rafael that Jordan must operate, if he is to succeed in blowing the bridge at the right time: there are no others.

Caring and killing

At the same time, Jordan has much else to think about. What is he to do about Maria, whom he has promised to care for? The republicans may no longer believe in marriage, just as they no longer officially believe in God: but they are far from happy that he should have taken their woman, and if he were to trifle with her they would kill him for it. Jordan would like to care for Maria for the rest of their lives, but

CHAPTER 3

the war must come first. After that, who knows? He cannot think so far ahead into the unknown. He will care for her for what may be the rest of their lives: the next 48 hours.

Hemingway is a serious writer and his characters do not avoid the big questions. Jordan would like to believe that he is on the side of right; that the killing is necessary in order to win the war; and that a republican victory will result in a better outcome for Spain. At the same time, he has doubts. To kill a man is wrong in itself, no matter what the cause; and not everyone whom he kills is a sincere and dedicated fascist. Many of his opponents are conscripts. Moreover, he has heard a first-hand, detailed and horrifying account by Pilar of how the republicans took control of the town of Avila and murdered the local fascists. They were led by Pablo, who took a cunning, sadistic and protracted pleasure in his work. He locked up the town's fascists in the town hall, and trickled them out one by one to be battered to death by a drunken and frenzied mob. Finally he became bored, and summoned the mob into the hall to finish the job.

Not all who were killed were dedicated fascists, and many of them did not deserve to die. Was Pablo later ashamed of his conduct of the operation, and did he ever regret what had occurred? In his own way, he did. He came to believe that how he had organised the execution was unprofessional; and he especially despised the behaviour of the priest, who died badly. Pilar was not surprised at this. Everyone dies badly, she says, and she adds:

> "I thought you hated priests."
>
> "Yes" said Pablo, and cut some more bread. "But a *Spanish* priest. A *Spanish* priest should die very well." (page 134)

Pilar was ashamed of what had occurred, but Pablo was not: and this was the side that he, Jordan, was supporting. The fascists might be equally brutal: but was there really anything to choose between the two sides? Jordan thought that there was, and he managed to cling to his belief: but he had his doubts.

CHAPTER 3

Narration

We have described Hemingway's style as terse. He tells this story in a reasonably laconic style, but not with the same economy of words as in his short story The Killers. This story is told by the author as 'omniscient narrator', in the third person; and as is usual with Hemingway, the action tells the story. However, in this case we are directly aware of Jordan's thoughts and feelings. He assesses and is critical of his own actions, and he discusses them with others whom he can trust, such as Anselmo and Pilar; but this is always after the event. Leadership is always lonely.

In For Whom the Bells Tolls, there are other changes of style. This is in part a love story and it is set in the Spanish culture as Hemingway reflects it. Thus, forms of speech are important. Spanish distinguishes between "you" and "thou" and so does Hemingway: the result appears archaic to an English reader, and requires an adjustment of mind. It is almost as if Hemingway regards the Spanish themselves as archaic, with their extraordinary pride and obstinacy; and he more than once describes Spain as a catholic but not a Christian country. Jordan, however, is almost as rigid in his views as the Spanish peasants who surround him. He objects when the older revolutionary, Pilar, addresses him formally (as "senor") and does not use the prefix 'comrade.' Jordan, the revolutionary by choice, insists on the proper style of informal address. Pilar is more relaxed, and has the greater sense of humour; she is capable of both mockery and irony, and does not devote her every waking thought to the revolution.

Does Hemingway's style work, in this novel? For this reader, only in part; and the lyrical passages are less successful than the hard-boiled prose with its reported speech. This is interspersed with obscenities which Hemingway, writing in 1940, could not translate directly, but is nevertheless effective. It is hard to convey the humour of a very different culture, as Hemingway attempts to do; and we cannot always be sure where the characters are intending irony. But that is to stray into literary criticism, which is not our preoccupation. The story is readable and the leadership issues arising are very clear.

CHAPTER 3

Leadership issues

Some of the leadership issues have already emerged as we have outlined aspects of the plot.

- ☐ Who is the leader, and what is the basis for his power?

Jordan is in a tricky position. Is he the leader of the group? If so, what is the basis for his power? To whom, or indeed to what, is he accountable? General Golz? Pilar? His fellow guerrillas? The spirit of the republic? His conscience? He has already answered this question, but it continues to torment him. He must obey orders. Golz's attack must succeed, in so far as Jordan is able to make it do so. It is his task to blow the bridge at the right time and everything else must be subordinated to that. He cannot waste his men and resources in attempting to save El Sordo, whom he sacrifices to his fate. He must kill Pablo, if need be. And he cannot protect Maria. His is the lonely choice of the reliable man; and he knows it.

- ☐ What is the relationship between leadership and gender?

Hemingway, the lover of the bull-fight and the high priest of machismo, is surprisingly undogmatic on this topic. Men do not necessarily make the best leaders, and leadership, even in Spain, is not a male prerogative. If Pilar has the right qualities for leadership, then let her be the leader: and she is acclaimed as such by the male members of the group. The Spanish may be traditionally-minded, but they are not stupid. As republicans, they are prepared to challenge tradition and overthrow prejudice; but there is a limit to how far they will go. We may note that the basic division of labour between men and women is sacrosanct and is never challenged by either sex. The men do not do the housework in the cave, and would be ridiculed by the women if they tried. There are no children in this story and the issue of caring for them does not arise. Perhaps we may assume that like Guiseppe Garibaldi's wife, Ana Ribeira da Silva, the true Spanish partisan would produce and raise her children whilst still wielding a rifle; but it is more likely that any children would be cared for elsewhere.

☐ When is violence justified, and to whom does it appeal too much?

As we have already seen, this is a difficult area. Jordan is not a pacifist—if he were, he would not be in the mountains in the first place—and he has accepted that violence is part of war and cannot always be limited. It worries him that some enjoy violence more than others, and that it can act as a drug; but its use cannot be avoided. It is right, however, that the subject should be discussed and worries raised: and the presence of those who look forward to killing is distasteful.

☐ Leadership and sacrifice

Jordan appears to be an atomic man, in the sense that he has no relatives or dependants. He is unmarried, his father committed suicide, and there is no mention of a mother or siblings. In other words, it would appear that Jordan has only himself to care for, and may throw away his life in the Spanish civil war if he chooses to do so.[5] He is not a reckless person, and appears to have calculated not only on surviving the war, but returning to his previous life afterwards: he had taken a year's absence from his duties as an instructor in Spanish at the University of Montana, and has reckoned on returning to this post. However, the war must come first and he will sacrifice himself if he has to do so. Will he also sacrifice others? We already know the answer to that question.

☐ The right to lead

The right to lead depends upon the ability to lead, and the potential leader must first of all be sure that he has the requisite knowledge, skills and qualities. Then he must put his opinion to the test of democratic acceptance. If he does become leader, then he may still attempt to consult with and sound out his followers as to the right course of action. However, he must have confidence in his own judgment, and act alone and without consultation when it is necessary to do so: although he may wish to check out the opinion of a trusted comrade afterwards. (Thus, Jordan listens to Pilar's opinion as to whether or not he did the right thing in deciding not to help El Sordo when he came under attack. She agrees. It was the right decision.) Above all, the leader must be honest with himself. If he made the wrong decision he must admit it to himself, so that his next decision will be a better one.

☐   The right to be there (at all)

This is an issue which might seem to apply solely to Robert Jordan, a volunteer who has chosen to take part in someone else's war, but it has a wider application. Moreover, it could be taken to precede all other considerations. Should he be in the mountains at all? Has he the right to take part in someone else's conflict? Jordan is an idealist, but that is not enough, for idealists can do harm as well as good—as was shown in Graham Greene's novel The Quiet American (Greene, 1955) which is set in Indo-China (now Vietnam). Graham Greene's quiet American, Alden Pyle, becomes involved in another country's troubles because he wishes to do good. He chooses to fulfil his ideals, however, in association with the CIA. His actions lead to the death of innocent people, and do not achieve the result for which he had hoped. Alden Pyle's idealism is dangerous, not only for himself (he is murdered) but for others.

Robert Jordan is in a different situation to Alden Pyle. In the first place, he is primarily risking his own life and not the lives of other people; and secondly, he has joined an organised and legitimate movement, which would have existed even had he not intervened. (As summarised earlier, the Spanish civil war began because General Franco invaded Spain in order to overthrow an elected government— although naturally he would have claimed otherwise. Therefore, it can be argued that the guerrillas represent legitimacy.)

Jordan may be preferable to Pyle, but that does not mean that his actions are justified.[6] Indeed, the person who is convinced that he is right and is prepared to sacrifice his own life to prove it, may be the most dangerous person of all. Suicide bombers believe in what they are doing, and are by definition prepared to sacrifice their own lives in doing it. That does not make their action right.

CHAPTER 3

The existential leader

Like all real-life moral dilemmas, Jordan's choice lends itself to more than one evaluation. Indeed, a moral dilemma is by definition a problem to which there is more than one 'right' solution. Is he right to take part in the Spanish struggle? There is no absolute rule that may be easily applied in this case, and the judgement of history cannot help him to make his decision beforehand. Jordan cannot know the long-term consequences of his actions: nor indeed what might have happened if he were not there and had not intervened.

His dilemma is an existential one, and Jordan acts as his nature prompts him to do. In doing so, he makes an initial choice which has other consequences, and he must face those as they arise. He has chosen to offer his services to the republic. He has chosen to work as an explosive expert. And he has chosen to be loyal to General Golz. (Golz is, like Jordan, is a stranger to Spain, and is moreover a Russian communist, with his own ideological baggage: but Jordan is loyal to him as his commanding officer. All military campaigns require obedience.) All of Jordan's choices have consequences, right down the causal chain; and he debates all of them, at least with himself.

In this analyst's view, Jordan's choice, or choices, are defensible rather than right in some absolute sense. Jordan commits himself to combat in the dust of the arena, rather than choosing to offer his opinion as an armchair philosopher. He is primarily risking his own life for a cause in which he believes; and he is attacking the enemy under the laws of war and not acting as a terrorist. If we accept that war can be a justified activity, then arguably he has a right to do so: and it would be unnatural, given the strength of his feelings, to act otherwise.

As Pablo sees very clearly, Jordan's intervention spells doom for his little group of partisans: but then, they had already agreed to fight, and had made that moral choice for themselves. Was Pablo entitled to change his mind? For himself, yes. For the group, no.

In a comparable situation, as a journalist who had gone out to 'cover' the Spanish civil war, George Orwell said that he joined the POUM (an anarchist group fighting as part of the anti-fascist alliance) because it seemed the obvious and natural thing to do. The really important decisions that we make in life are not necessarily the ones over which we linger the longest, and in some cases they may not feel like decisions at all. Jordan has recognised that his efforts will neither be recognised nor rewarded: except by those whose opinion he values.

Conclusion

As we may see from the quotations from John McCain that are included in this chapter, Ernest Miller Hemingway was someone who wrote about leaders as he felt that they ought to be, not only to inspire the admiration of his readers for his literary skills, but to make them into better leaders themselves. Robert Jordan, the hero of A Farewell to Arms, is in John McCain's opinion everything a leader ought to be. We do not disagree with that assessment, which seems to go beyond an American view of leadership to something approaching a universal ideal.

Questions for reflection

- What are Robert Jordan's strengths and weaknesses, as a leader?
- How should he address the difficulty that he is not in official command of the group?
- What should he have done about Pablo?
- What does Pilar have to offer, as a leader?
- What does this story tell you about leadership, outside the context of the Spanish civil war?
- Do you share John McCain's admiration for Robert Jordan?

□ We wrote earlier that 'leadership is always lonely', meaning that the leader will sometimes need to face and make decisions that may make him very unpopular with his group. What are your views on this? Does leadership require moral courage, and is it necessarily 'lonely at the top'? What is your own experience of the isolating effect of being the leader? How might that sense of isolation be reduced, without compromising integrity?

Commentary on questions

□ What are Robert Jordan's strengths and weaknesses, as a leader?

The first four questions are answerable, we believe, from analysis of the material offered in the chapter, whereas the last three questions go wider.

Robert Jordan appears an almost perfect leader, and part of his perfection, if we may be paradoxical, is that he has flaws: for if he were too perfect he would not be human. His strengths are almost too numerous to cite. He is courageous, determined, level-headed and pragmatic, and works from the situation as it is, and not how it might be. It is a possible weakness that he fails to deal with the issue of Pablo's loyalty as soon as he might: in a guerrilla band in which leadership is disputed, ruthlessness in taking command is not necessarily an undesirable characteristic.

□ How should he address the difficulty that he is not in official command of the group?

This is addressed in the text. Jordan shows determination, strategic insight, technical skill, and general qualities of character that are more than enough to compensate for his unofficial status in the group, and make him its natural leader.

□ What should he have done about Pablo?

We believe that he should have taken action sooner, and shot him.

- What does Pilar have to offer, as a leader?

Again, as the text demonstrates, a great deal. She has a quality of humanity that is lacking in the rather humourless Jordan.

- What does this story tell you about leadership, outside the context of the Spanish civil war?

We believe that the lessons on leadership that are shown in this text may be applied in a much wider context than that of war. Leadership requires justified self-confidence: the ability to share decision-making, if on occasion by retrospective endorsement; and the capacity to go against the mood of the group when necessary, provided that the leader is ultimately able to lead his followers in a new and successful direction. The leader must focus on the essential task at hand, and make sure that it is accomplished—but not at the expense of destroying the team or alienating its members.

Action-centred leadership

John Adair asserts that it is the enduring task of the leader to achieve a balance between three sometimes conflicting priorities:

1. To achieve the task;
2. To build the team; and
3. To develop its individuals.

The theory of action-centred leadership is a permanent contribution to leadership doctrine, and is worthy of application in any real-life context where a leadership dilemma presents itself.

- Do you share John McCain's admiration for Robert Jordan?

As a personal preference, we do. Is it not rather odd, to express an admiration for a fictional person? At the expense of sounding like a philosophical relativist, we should argue that on this occasion it is valid to assert that Robert Jordan is real—for John McCain; and that it is a fundamental tenet of this book to show that leadership as shown in literature may have a real influence on real people.

> ☐ We wrote earlier that 'leadership is always lonely', meaning that the leader will sometimes need to face and make decisions that may make him very unpopular with his group. What are your views on this? Does leadership require moral courage, and is it necessarily 'lonely at the top'? What is your own experience of the isolating effect of being the leader? How might that sense of isolation be reduced, without compromising integrity?

These are questions, we would suggest, that are best addressed within a group that has achieved an effective level of confidentiality. We have yet to read an account of leadership which does not refer to the loneliness of command, or the difficulty of sharing the problems that the leader must address. We would suggest that there is a difference between being unable to share a problem because its solution rests on the use of confidential information, and being unwilling to share a problem because the leader wishes to project an image of infallibility: he is the sort of person who does not need to discuss or share issues, because he always knows the right answer. If the leader does believe that, then we would suggest that he is confusing leadership with egotism.

Notes

1   Although Ernest Hemingway and George Orwell were in Paris (and later Spain) at the same time, the two writers never met. Orwell, the austere and ascetic Old Etonian who had determined to see life at the bottom, was working as a dish-washer in a fourth rate hotel, and made no literary acquaintances: although he could have found Hemingway and his acquaintances easily enough, for they usually frequented a well-known café as a well-known group. Orwell was to write a vivid description of his experience in his book, Down and Out in Paris and London. The title was an accurate one.

2   This account of the Spanish civil war is intended purely as a précis of an event that deserves at least a book of its own. Hemingway's novel, For Whom The Bell Tolls, if read in full, is an effective portrayal of the reality of the conflict

CHAPTER 3

between Nationalists and Republicans, which recognises that virtue was not all on one side.

3   This was a mixed blessing, as many commentators have pointed out. The Soviet Union was more concerned with supporting the Spanish communists than ensuring the re-establishment of the Spanish Republic, and did not in any case provide unlimited aid. George Orwell, in his book A Homage to Catalonia, points out that the Russian forces helped to promote a civil war within a civil war, as the communists fought against the anarchists.

4   Cuba was ruled by the military dictator Fulgencio Batista, who was overthrown by Fidel Castro in 1956. Batista was linked to some very dubious people in the United States, and Cuba was to some extent a haven for gangsters on vacation. Hemingway, however, seems to have simply regarded it as a place where he could be free to fish and to write. He is reported to have welcomed Castro's assumption of power: but he was to return to live in the United States at the end of the decade.

5   Compare the moral dilemmas raised in Jean Paul Sartre's fictional works, which bring to life his existentialist philosophy. In one instance, a young student in Nazi-occupied France faces a profound dilemma. Should he join the resistance, which is what he wants to do, or continue to support his widowed mother, who has no other source of support? Both options can be argued for, on moral grounds; but no moral argument will resolve his existentialist dilemma.
Sartre's plays include Les Mains Sales (1948), translated into English by Kitty Black as Crime Passionel, which deals with a young man who needs to carry out an assassination, but, like Hamlet, is reluctant to do so.
On the face of it, Ernest Hemingway the American man of action and Jean-Paul Sartre the French intellectual would appear to have had little in common, apart from a predilection for living in Paris; but there is a resonance in the issues they address.

6   The soldier who participates in a foreign conflict not as a mercenary but as a sympathetic volunteer does not thereby remove himself from moral scrutiny, and some of the arguments that relate to the criteria for a just war also apply in his case. In other words, the impulse to support a cause in which a person passionately believes does not necessarily justify his participation, and nor does his selflessness in doing so.
Compare the doctor who risks his own life, in order to find out whether a new drug, technique or operation may be successful or not. (He might, for example, test a drug on himself if there appears no other way of testing its efficacy.) Such a person would appear capable of performing a perfect act of disinterested virtue: but even in this case, we would suggest that his motives are not irrelevant.

CHAPTER 4

Leadership and bureaucracy: Joseph Conrad and *The Secret Agent*

Joseph Conrad (1857 to 1924) was a remarkable person and a remarkable writer. He showed an extraordinary facility for being ahead of his time and for addressing enduring issues, and his work is full of lessons on leadership. In Leadership and Literature (Triarchy Press, 2011) we explore in depth the leadership lessons to be derived from a selection of Conrad's sea literature. Here, we shall explore his penetrating analysis of espionage and its lessons for leadership[1].

Conrad: exile, sailor and writer

Jozef Teodor Konrad Korzeniowski was born in 1857 to a Polish family resident in the Ukraine. The once powerful kingdom of Poland had been dismembered by its neighbours three times, and in 1795, under the third partition of Poland, it had officially ceased to exist. What had been Poland was divided under Prussian, Russian and Austrian rule; and although Conrad was ethnically a Pole and Polish was his first language, by birth he was a Russian subject.

Conrad's father, Apollo Korzeniowski (1820-1869) was an ardent patriot who was convicted of conspiracy and sent into exile in northern Russia in 1862, together with his frail young wife and their only child. The exile was a disaster from which the family never recovered. Ewa became so ill with tuberculosis that she was finally allowed to return to Poland to die. She did so in 1865, to be followed to the grave four years later by her mourning husband.

Konrad Korzeniowski—a name he was not to change until he became a published author under another nationality—became the ward of his uncle, Tadeusz Bobrowski. The adolescent Conrad expressed a strong determination to go to sea, and joined the French merchant service in Marseilles in 1874. Four years later he transferred to the British

CHAPTER 4

merchant service. He served under the Red Ensign until 1894, largely under sail. He obtained his master mariner's certificate in sail in 1886 and his only command, the barque Otago, in 1888. Conrad visited the Belgian Congo under contract to command a river paddle-steamer in 1890; this later resulted in perhaps his best known work, the novella Heart of Darkness.

By the age of 36, Conrad's merchant service career was in the doldrums, and he had begun to write. (In fact, he had been working intermittently on what was to become his first novel, Almayer's Folly, for the past five years). Within less than two years, he had published Almayer's Folly, married a Miss Jessie George, and settled ashore to pursue a new career as a writer—the result of a combination of circumstances, perhaps, rather than a planned strategy. Despite the doubts and misgivings which were an inescapable part of his character, and the financial difficulties he faced which were on occasion almost overwhelming, Conrad continued with the struggle to produce his exceptional works in his third language. He was awarded critical appreciation from the start, but financial success was to elude him until Chance was published in 1913.

Conrad died in 1924, the acclaimed author of a number of highly respected novels which were held to be in the vanguard of literary modernism, notable especially for the dazzling switches of viewpoint and voice in his multi-layered narratives. It would be a mistake to confine his impact to any one period or style. His influence is with us still, and we live in a world on which Conrad's perspective remains relevant. Indeed, the philosopher John Gray has called him Conrad, our contemporary: and The Secret Agent tells us why.

The Secret Agent

This 1907 novel is a product of Conrad's imagination, stimulated by a real event—an anarchist outrage in Greenwich Park. In the Penguin Classic (centenary) edition of The Secret Agent (2007), the introduction by Michael Newton begins:

> 'On the afternoon of 15 February 1894, a twenty-six-year-old Frenchman named Martial Bourdin left Fitzroy Street, in

central London, and travelled south-east towards Greenwich Park, at the city's margins. A tram driver noticed that something appeared to be in the young man's pocket. Later a park-keeper saw Bourdin walking among the trees, holding a small brown paper parcel. He was heading towards the path that led to the Greenwich Observatory. Somewhere out of sight he unwrapped the package and discarded the paper. Inside was a bomb. As he walked on, it suddenly exploded. Bourdin's injuries were fatal. He was conscious for a while, although in terrible pain; he died before reaching hospital.'

From this brief and never explained incident, Conrad assembled a masterpiece of irony about the world in which he lived. The Secret Agent is not a simple tale of good and evil, and it has no hero. Indeed, Conrad finds the anarchists, the police who pursue them, and the politicians to whom those police officers report, to be equally unworthy of admiration. The anarchists, in fact, are almost beneath contempt, although Conrad does express a sort of reluctant admiration for their explosives expert, the Professor—the only zealot amongst them.

Plot and characters: The reviewer's dilemma

The plot of The Secret Agent does not lend itself to an easy summary, for this is no ordinary thriller, and Conrad does not follow a conventional chronological sequence. Moreover, we do not wish to spoil the story; and we have therefore offered only enough of the plot to illuminate our purpose in this book. What follows, therefore, is incomplete, but is not intended to be exasperating. We begin where the book begins, with the meeting of a secret agent, Mr Verloc, with his new handler at the Russian embassy in London in the early 1900s.

Mr Verloc and Mr Vladimir

In middle age, Mr Verloc is both massive and passive, at least as far as the expenditure of physical energy is concerned: for he is incurably indolent. He is accustomed to breakfast in bed, 'and (to) remain wallowing there with an air of quiet enjoyment until noon every day—and sometimes even to a later hour.' (page 6). His most notable

CHAPTER 4

characteristic is his voice, a profound bass capable of being heard at a great distance, and highly suitable for demagoguery: for Mr Verloc, like any other craftsman, takes a pride in his professional skills. Mr Verloc is a secret agent with two masters: the London police and the Russian embassy,[2] where Mr Vladimir is the First Secretary. Something of a society favourite, and an honorary member of several leading clubs, this plump and smiling official is in reality a relentless and cynical task-master. He is determined to alert European society to the danger within their midst—by creating himself, what they will most fear. In his first meeting with Mr Verloc he sets out to shock his complacency, and then proceeds to set him a new sort of task.

> '"You understand French, I suppose?" He said.
>
> Mr Verloc stated huskily that he did... At once, with contemptuous perversity, Mr Vladimir changed the language, and began to speak idiomatic English without the trace of a foreign accent.' (page 24)

Ruthless as he is, Mr Vladimir has two weaknesses. Firstly he fails to understand what he is dealing with, as Verloc soon realises. '(And) Mr Vladimir developed his idea (for an anarchist outrage) from on high, with scorn and condescension, displaying at the same time an amount of ignorance as to the real aims, thoughts and methods of the revolutionary world which filled the silent Mr Verloc with inward consternation.' (page 24) Secondly, the apparently intrepid Mr Vladimir has a morbid fear of the police. 'Descended from generations victimised by the instruments of an arbitrary power, he was racially, nationally and individually afraid of the police. It was an inherited weakness, altogether independent of his judgment, of his reason, of his experience. He was born to it. But that sentiment, which resembled the irrational horror some people have of cats, did not stand in the way of his immense contempt for the English police.' (page 178) Despite his talents, however, Mr Vladimir proves to be no match for his opponent, the Assistant Commssioner, who outwits him comprehensively.

Mr Verloc is a married man, who has another occupation besides that of secret agent: he is a shop-keeper who deals in pornography. Both occupations are far from respectable and take place in an atmosphere

CHAPTER 4

of secrecy and deception. Both are officially illegal. Both are to some extent tolerated by the police, either as a lesser evil or for the information that they may provide for the authorities. Finally, neither requires very much work on the part of Mr Verloc.

As the story begins, Mr Verloc has been summoned to the embassy that employs him on a clandestine basis. Mr Vladimir, the new First Secretary, is severely displeased with his secret agent, who has not been doing enough to justify his keep; and commands him to act as an agent provocateur. His target is science: he is to blow up the Royal Observatory at Greenwich.

Mr Verloc is horrified, but has little choice but to comply, for his work as a secret agent is his only real source of income. However, the far from intrepid secret agent has a practical problem; for the anarchists with whom he is in touch are either unwilling or unable (with one significant exception) to put their ideas into practice, and to assist in the actual planting of a bomb.

The Future of the Proletariat: Michaelis, Yundt and Ossipon

We first meet the anarchists on whom Mr Verloc offers his secret reports when three of them have assembled in his parlour, and Michaelis is addressing his comrades Yundt and Ossipon on the subject of history. Mr Verloc is in attendance, and his wife's simple brother Stevie is within earshot. Mrs Verloc, who preserves her inscrutability for much of the story, appears to be paying no attention to what is going on; whereas Stevie will be excited by any reference to oppression and cruelty. Stevie is very easily excited; and once he has become excited, it is very difficult to restore him to equanimity.

Michaelis

> 'Michaelis, the ticket-of-leave apostle[3], was speaking in an even voice, a voice that wheezed as if deadened and oppressed by the layer of fat on his chest. He had come out of a highly hygienic prison round like a tub, with an enormous stomach and distended cheeks of a pale, semi-transparent complexion, as though for fifteen years the servants of an outraged society

CHAPTER 4

had made a point of stuffing him with fattening foods in a damp and lightless cellar. And ever since he had never managed to get his weight down as much as an ounce[4].' (page 33)

Yundt

If Michaelis is a holy fool, Yundt is purely malicious. He giggles grimly, 'with a faint black grimace of a toothless mouth. The terrorist, as he called himself, was old and bald, with a narrow, snow-white wisp of a goatee hanging limply from his chin. An extraordinary expression of underhand malevolence survived in his extinguished eyes. When he rose painfully the thrusting forward of a skinny groping hand deformed by gouty swellings suggested the effort of a moribund murderer summoning all his remaining strength for a last stab.' (page 34)

However, in reality 'the famous terrorist had never in his life raised personally as much as his little finger against the social edifice. He was no man of action... (but) took the part of an insolent and venomous evoker of sinister impulses... The shadow of his evil gift clung to him yet like the smell of a deadly drug in an old vial of poison, emptied now, useless, ready to be thrown away on the rubbish-heap of things that had served their time.' (page 39)

Ossipon

The third member of the unholy triumvirate who, with Mr Verloc himself, constitute the vanguard of the Future of the Proletariat, is Alexander Ossipon. Young, tall and robust, with a mass of curly yellow hair atop his flattened features, he looks like a Norwegian sailor who has just been on a spree. In fact, Comrade Ossipon is a failed medical student who believes himself to be a scientist, and is deeply attached to the theories of the criminologist Cesare Lombroso (1835-1909), which he uses to label Stevie as an obvious degenerate. He writes pamphlets[5], for which he receives a small sum; but his real occupation is preying on the affections of naive and foolish girls, whom he is able to detach from their savings by a combination of flattery and false promises. The parasitic Ossipon is horrified when the unexpected bombing in Greenwich Park threatens his idle and comfortable existence.

The Professor

The professor does not participate in the proceedings of the Future of the Proletariat, since he heartily despises them and in any case prefers to work alone. He is a dingy little man in spectacles (page 49), but nevertheless a figure of unease for the special crimes section of the police, who know that he is always prepared to blow himself up. The professor is a walking bomb, who tells his fellow anarchist, Ossipon, that 'I walk always with my right hand closed round the India-rubber ball which I have in my trouser pocket. The pressing of this ball actuates a detonator inside the flask in my pocket. It's the principle of the pneumatic instantaneous shutter for a camera lens.' (page 53) He shows the horrified Ossipon that he is indeed 'wired up'; and confirms that when he squeezes the ball, there will be a twenty second delay until the explosion, which will blow everyone within a certain distance to smithereens.

In contrast with the 'lamentable inferiority of his physique' (page 50) the 'professor' (in reality, a one-time chemistry demonstrator) has a supremely self-confident bearing and a particularly impressive manner of keeping silent. All his movements have an assured precision, and he is absolutely sure of what he is doing. His intention in life is to make the perfect detonator, and as an anarchist, he is prepared to supply that or any other explosive product to anyone who asks for it—as he informs Comrade Ossipon in his usual curt way. (page 51)

> "'My absolute rule is never to refuse anybody—as long as I have a pinch (of explosives) by me," answered the little man with decision.
>
> "That's a principle?" Commented Ossipon.
>
> "That's a principle."
>
> "And you think it's sound?"

CHAPTER 4

> The large round spectacles, which gave a look of staring self-confidence to the sallow face, confronted Ossipon like sleepless, unwinking orbs flashing a cold fire.
>
> "Perfectly. Always. Under every circumstance. What could stop me? Why should I not? Why should I think twice about it?" (page 52)

Nothing would please the professor more than to be shot down in the street by the forces of law and order like a mad dog; for that would show the bourgeosie that the supposedly liberal and civilised society which they like to believe surrounds them is in reality nothing but a sham. The professor is afraid of no-one and nothing: except that his efforts should pass unnoticed. He is the only one of the anarchists for whom Conrad, as author, shows any respect; for he is the only one who really believes in what he is doing.

Mr Verloc is able to obtain the explosives he needs from the professor, who assembles a time-delay bomb for him, using a soldered can for a container. Verloc coaches his brother-in-law Stevie to be the deliverer of the engine of destruction. Why Stevie? Firstly, he is expendable. Secondly, if he should somehow be arrested, the police will be unable to learn anything useful from him; for he will be loyal to his mentor, Mr Verloc, whom he knows to be 'good.'

However, Mr Verloc's attempt to provide a 'spectacular' which is capable of shocking middle-class opinion results only in the destruction of his mentally challenged brother-in-law, who stumbles over the roots of a tree and blows himself up—leaving only fragments to be gathered together by a stolid constable and examined on a table top by the reluctant but always professionally-minded Chief Inspector Heat—who will receive his own introduction in the next section.

> "'You used a shovel,'" (Heat) remarked, observing a sprinkling of small gravel, tiny brown bits of bark, and particles of splintered wood as fine as needles.
>
> "Had to in one place," said the stolid constable. "I sent a keeper to fetch a spade. When he heard me scraping the ground with it he leaned his forehead against a tree, and was as sick as a dog." (page 70)

CHAPTER 4

The process of unravelment

As we have already indicated, the story of The Secret Agent is not related in chronological order, and is not revealed from a universal perspective. By contrast, and rather as in real life, each participant in the story gradually learns more of what is going on and alters his or her perspective accordingly. Thus, when the bomb explodes, only Mr Verloc can be reasonably sure of the identity of its victim. Even he does not know this for certain, for when he hears the explosion occur prematurely (that is, before Stevie could have reached the agreed objective, which he had been left to do on his own), he assumes the worst and hurries from the park as fast as he can. His fears are later confirmed; but not before other people are also in possession of part of the truth.

Both police and anarchists alike wish to know who planted the bomb, for they share an interest in restoring public tranquillity: but they go about finding out what has happened in different ways. Chief Inspector Heat has the advantage that he is able to make an official investigation. Entirely by chance, he is able to identify the body: for Mrs Verloc has identified her brother's clothing by sewing in a name-tag, without informing her husband of her sensible precaution. This is a piece of information that Heat keeps to himself, for in his world knowledge is power.

When Mrs Verloc learns of what has happened, as a result of a police visit to the shop, her reaction is twofold. Firstly, she is devastated by the death of her brother. Secondly, she realises that she no longer need remain married to Mr Verloc; for it was in order to obtain his protection for her brother (and mother) that she agreed to marry him in the first place. Her mother has already gone, and Stevie's death has set her free; but she does not know what to do with her freedom.

CHAPTER 4

The special crimes section and its officials: Chief Inspector Heat

The special crimes section of the London police[6] falls under the command of an Assistant Commissioner. Its driving force, however, is Chief Inspector Heat; and so adept is he at his job that he has been consulted, on occasion, directly by the Home Secretary, who has thereby by-passed the official commander of the section.

Heat is an old departmental hand, who has his own way of doing things, and whose loyalty, in the opinion of his superior officer, should not be pushed too far. He is a little too proud of his abilities, and his professional arrogance leads him to make mistakes. Conscious that he is the expert within his department, he had given an assurance that no outbreak of anarchist activity was to be expected — less than a week before the Greenwich bombing actually occurred.

It is an essential part of the reputation of a senior police officer to be a reliable source of knowledge; and he can make no greater mistake than to give a false assurance, for once his credibility has been weakened it will be very hard to regain it. As Conrad puts it, Heat 'had gone even so far as to utter words [to the Home Secretary in person] which true wisdom would have kept back. But Chief Inspector Heat was not so very wise — at least not truly so. True wisdom, which is not certain of anything in this world of contradictions, would have prevented him from obtaining his present position.' (page 67) [7]

Chief Inspector Heat has a comfort zone, which is to deal with ordinary criminals such as thieves, for whom he feels something 'not very far removed from affection.' (page 73) Heat 'could understand the mind of a burglar, because, as a matter of fact, the mind and the instincts of a burglar are of the same kind as the mind and instincts of a police officer. Both recognise the same conventions, and have a working knowledge of each other's methods and of the routine of their respective trades. They understand each other, which is advantageous to both, and establishes a sort of amenity in their relations.' (page 74)

Heat's comfort zone does not include anarchists, and in particular the professor, who arouses in him a profound unease: not only for the very real danger that he presents but because of his profound contempt for everything the chief inspector holds dear.

Heat has an informer, a secret agent named Verloc whose continued work is far more important to him than any other priority, legal or ethical, and whose services he shares with a foreign power. Although he realises that Verloc has instigated the bombing in Greenwich Park in his reluctant role as agent provocateur, Heat is perfectly prepared to manipulate the evidence so that another and innocent man, Michaelis, will be convicted—and the indispensable Verloc will remain his informer.

The Assistant Commissioner

The Assistant Commissioner (who is never named) is a tall, lean[8] man who, according to Mrs Verloc, looks distinctly foreign. There is a suggestion of Don Quixote about his appearance, but there is nothing quixotic in his behaviour. This Don Quixote does not tilt at windmills, but confines his attention to real targets. He has a background in colonial policing, and married somewhat impulsively whilst on long leave in England. However, he was to discover that his new wife had no intention of living in a colony, and he has had to take employment in London. His work is largely administrative, and he has no chance to exercise his detective skills—except on his own subordinates, whom he rightly suspects of concealing things from him which they believe that he does not need to know.

> 'The head of the so-called Special Crimes Department, debarred by his position from going out personally in quest of secrets locked up in guilty breasts, had a propensity to exercise his considerable gifts for the detection of incriminating truth on his own subordinates... (His detective skill) fed, since it could not roam abroad, upon the human material which was brought to it in its official seclusion. We can never cease to be ourselves.' (page 94)

His official subordinate, Heat, is a highly successful and respected police officer; but his main preoccupation, as his Assistant Commissioner reflects, appears to be to keep his senior officer in the dark about what is really going on. Part of the challenge to the Assistant Commissioner's leadership, therefore, is to find a means to ensure that

CHAPTER 4

it is he and not his subordinate, who is running the department; and part of the pleasure of following the plot of this subtle and carefully constructed novel is to observe how he is able to do so.

Almost as a matter of professional instinct, the Assistant Commissioner has no intention of allowing Heat to pull the wool over his eyes. He might then be blamed for something which was outside his knowledge and therefore beyond his control; and in any case he enjoys the thrill of the chase. As Conrad puts it:

> 'His nature was one that is not easily accessible to illusions. He knew that a department is at the mercy of its subordinate officers, who have their own conception of loyalty...' (page 79)

He interrogates Heat, and forces him to reveal that he knows the identity of the man whose remains had been discovered in Greenwich Park that morning. Having admitted to this, Heat gloomily decides, as a last resort, to tell his boss everything; and the Assistant Commissioner learns of the existence and use of Mr Verloc as an unofficial and unregistered police informer, to whose services Chief Inspector Heat had obtained access almost by chance.

The Assistant Commissioner behaves with great perspicacity. Firstly, he makes contact with the Home Secretary himself (for the first time) and informs him of what he has discovered, and why he intends to make a personal intervention. Then, he prepares himself for some real police work, disguising his appearance, taking a hasty meal at an Italian restaurant (which Conrad satirizes, en passant, as a remarkably British institution) and going to call on Mr Verloc himself — taking care to avoid the attention of any patrolling police constables as he does so. He reports back to the Home Secretary. Finally, he takes advantage of a chance encounter with Mr Vladimir, the darling of society, to exploit the information that he has gained and to threaten to expose Mr Vladimir's undiplomatic activities in using an agent provocateur. The Assistant Commissioner has triumphed over everyone but his wife; and can truly reflect that in this day's work he has earned his salary.

Commentary

The Secret Agent is a tale of conspiracy and deception in which nothing is what it seems and there are no heroes, although there are clearly victims: for this is no simple thriller. It is a tale suffused in irony, in which everyone has a hidden agenda and no-one's motives for his actions will stand up to very much investigation—although we may note that Conrad treats some of his characters, like the anarchists, with an ironic scorn, and others, like Mrs Verloc, with an ironic pity. It deals with the reality of leadership in the political arena, in which power rests upon the manipulation of information, and it is both right and proper to assume that no-one can be trusted; and it may be read to-day with the same rueful delight as when it was first published.

The ubiquity of deception

Almost everyone practices deception in this story, with the exception of Stevie who is too simple to do so. That deception may be either selfish or selfless: but it prevails. Mrs Verloc hides from her husband her reasons for marrying him: which are that he will look after her mother and brother, whereas the young man she loved would have been unable to do so. Mrs Verloc's mother hides from her daughter her reasons for seeking another home, which she is able to obtain through a benevolent society: she believes that the burden of looking after both his wife's mother and her brother will prove too much for Mr Verloc, and bring an end to the marriage. Both women, in other words, are prepared to sacrifice themselves for others' welfare; and both conceal their real motives from those they deceive.

Unless we believe that no deception is ever justified—a belief that would surely make normal life very difficult—then we must distinguish between kinds of deception, and decide which lies are morally justified [9]. If we apply this logic to 'The Secret Agent', then some deceptions are clearly more justified than others. But this story is set in a context in which deception is the norm, and in which people are expected to deceive one another, especially in their working relationships. Mr Verloc, as a secret agent with two masters, leads a life suffused in deception. That deception is extended even to his wife, in whom he has never confided: and when he finally decides to do so, it is too late. Chief Inspector Heat, who has his own conception of loyalty, routinely deceives his senior officer. He could plead in mitigation that it is his job to make sure that the section is an effective one, and he must be given a certain discretion in ensuring its success. That discretion, in Heat's view, extends a very long way, and includes the perversion of justice.

Scapegoating

When Heat finds out the identity of the dead man and the almost certain involvement of Mr Verloc in this outrage, his inclination is to pin the blame elsewhere: for it would very much suit the chief inspector to keep Verloc as his informer. However, he needs a scapegoat for the crime, in order to reassure the public as to the competence of the police in protecting them from the iniquities of anarchism. The obvious scapegoat is Michaelis, with whom Stevie had been staying until just before the explosion. No-one, including the chief inspector, really believes that Michaelis had anything to do with this crime, since he is happily preoccupied in writing his memoirs; but that is beside the point. Michaelis does not know anything, and therefore cannot reveal anything which could embarrass the police—as Verloc could certainly do if he were arrested. Moreover, Michaelis is on ticket-of-leave, and can easily be recalled to prison to complete his original sentence: and Heat is astute enough to have press contacts who will whip up public hatred against him. Therefore, and despite his almost certain innocence, he must be sacrificed to expediency.

It would be pleasant for those who believe in the intrinsic goodness of human nature to learn that the Assistant Commissioner is determined to save Michaelis because of his innocence. That, however, is not the Assistant Commissioner's motive. We may infer, from the few clues placed carefully in the text, that the Assistant Commissioner's marriage is not a happy one, and that his wife is not an easy person to please. She has a patroness, a great lady of society who is also the patroness of Michaelis; and were that convict to be returned to prison, then the Assistant Commissioner would be held to blame for his persecution. He puts this thought to himself with his customary precision.

"Damn it! If that infernal Heat has his way the fellow'll die in prison smothered in his own fat, and she'll never forgive me." (page 90)

Conrad shows a masterly insight into the world of the secret agent and his controllers, and into the political intrigues underlying terrorist atrocities. However, this is not 'escapist' literature and there are neither real heroes nor villains within it. It is a tale suffused in irony, in which everyone has a hidden agenda, and no-one's motives for their actions will stand up to very much investigation; and it deals with the reality of the kind of leadership in which power rests upon the manipulation of information.

Conrad, the exiled Pole whose parents had died as a punishment for their patriotism and who dismissed Christianity as an oriental fable, supported neither the establishment nor its opponents[10]. He was a man without illusions; and the most his leaders are allowed is a certain professional expertise. His book was not well received when first published, since it appeared both cynical and destructive. However, as the philosopher John Gray has noted (Gray, 2004), a later generation may take a different view. The Polish exile who rose to the rank of master mariner in sail, and who claimed that as a member of the Polish landed gentry he had no need of a British knighthood, is (in Gray's phrase) our contemporary.

Conrad and leadership

The main lessons of The Secret Agent as a parable of leadership, relate to the role and activities of the Assistant Commissioner of Police who is head of the special crimes section, and the maxims, which are never stated but always inferable, that he has to apply in becoming head of his department in reality as well as in name. What are those maxims?

Knowledge is power

Firstly, the AC needs to find out what is going on in reality, and not to rely on the voluntary co-operation of his subordinates in providing the information that he needs. Chief Inspector Heat, the effective head of the department until the AC was appointed, has his own concept of loyalty and his own way of doing things; and his actions are primarily intended to benefit Chief Inspector Heat. Should his new boss let sleeping dogs lie? Should he put his feet up, as it were, and enjoy what is in effect a sinecure? He would be most unwise to do so. It is against his nature; it may work against his own career interests; and it is not a strategic policy, for the chief inspector operates at a tactical level, and is therefore bound to come unstuck at some point.

Heat has self-confidence, drive and determination, and these qualities have helped to place him where he is. (In leadership theory, they are often recognised as desirable qualities in a leader. That may be true; but if generally desirable, they are certainly not sufficient qualities for good leadership.) As Conrad points out, Heat is a little too confident, and lacks the true wisdom of the person who does not exaggerate his knowledge. Heat's judgement is not at the same level as his executive abilities, and he should not be given overall responsibility for the department.

Judgement is vital

The AC arrives in his department, it would appear, an ignoramus as to its true workings, and has to find out for himself what is really going on. Having discovered the role of Mr Verloc as an informer, his dual relationship with both Chief Inspector Heat and Mr Vladimir, and his use as an agent provocateur, the AC needs to decide what to do about it; and he decides upon a softly, softly approach. The AC proceeds to form his own link with the Home Secretary, and to negotiate a solution to the real security issue facing London, which is that of meddling by foreign powers[11]. The Home Secretary recognises his skills and accepts his actions; and the AC has both consolidated his own position and shown the usefulness of his department. Heat is still in place, so that the AC will continue to be able to make use of his knowledge and skills; but he has been by-passed and is no longer a threat, real or potential, to his senior officer.

Grand moral principles have little place in 'realpolitik'

The AC operates in the world of realpolitik, and does not seek to apply highfalutin moral principles in his work, but rather a sort of intelligent self-interest. It is not for him to judge his chief subordinate from a moral perspective, but to decide how to make best use of him. His task as a police officer is to decide whom to support and whom to control, and not who is right or wrong; and he has little concern for grand, overarching principles — the rhetoric of politics, but not the reality. (Thus, as we have seen, he does not seek to protect the convict Michaelis from further conviction because it would be unjust, but because his wife would never forgive him.)

Extrapolation

How does The Secret Agent relate to the dilemmas facing the contemporary leader or manager, and what are we entitled to infer about the practice of leadership from this novel? Readers will already have begun to draw their own inferences: and we would suggest that the questions for reflection that accompany this chapter are a source for further reflection, whether for the reader alone or in group consideration and discussion.

Questions for reflection

- If every group has a leader, who is the leader of the group of anarchists in this story?

- The Assistant Commissioner of Police has a special crimes unit under his command, directed by the highly professional Chief Inspector Heat. Heat has a duty to keep his superior officer informed of what he needs to know. Why, then, does the Assistant Commissioner take it upon himself to make his own inquiries as to what is going on?

CHAPTER 4

- Which aspects of his work does the Assistant Commissioner enjoy, and what does he find frustrating? What should he do about it?

- To what extent does power rest upon the manipulation of information? Is this axiom unique to the security services, or does it also apply elsewhere?

- It was stated in the text that life without the occasional lie or other act of deception would be very difficult to sustain (whether at home or at work). What are your views on this? Is lying always wrong, no matter what the motives of the liar, or the demands of the situation? Have you ever been asked, at work, for information that you did not feel entitled to reveal, and if, so, how did you deal with the situation? Is a leader ever entitled to lie or practise deception, and if so, when and how?

- Conrad describes Chief Inspector Heat as not truly wise, in that he allows himself to give an assurance (that no terrorist outrage is about to occur in London) which is very soon falsified by events. On the other hand, Heat has been concerned to project an image of himself as both knowledgeable and confident of his own abilities: a reliable person who deserves his position. He should not have made an assurance that he could not guarantee; but we may understand why he did so. Have you ever been asked to provide an assurance when you did not feel fully confident or competent to do so, and if so, how did you deal with the situation?

- Do you feel that it is the task of the leader to raise the moral tone, as it were, and to refer to grand moral principles as applying to the everyday work of the organisation? Or is it better to operate in the world of *realpolitik*, to accept human nature for what it is, and to seek for pragmatic solutions to practical difficulties as they arise?

CHAPTER 4

Commentary on questions

☐ If every group has a leader, who is the leader of the group of anarchists in this story?

An anarchist group, almost by definition, should practise democratic decision-making: and the Future of the Proletariat has neither a formal leader nor an informal substitute. Yundt is too old, Ossipon too self-interested, and Michaelis, after twenty years of soliary confinement, is too far removed from ordinary life, to play the role of the leader. Verloc himself can play a leading role on occasion, because of his impressive voice; but as a police informer he is accustomed to playing a secondary role. That leaves the professor, who could be a leader—he has the determination, the technical expertise, and the quality of defiance—but prefers to operate alone. Perhaps every group does not have a leader, after all.

☐ The Assistant Commissioner of Police has a special crimes unit under his command, directed by the highly professional Chief Inspector Heat. Heat has a duty to keep his superior officer informed of what he needs to know. Why, then, does the Assistant Commissioner take it upon himself to make his own inquiries as to what is going on?

The AC makes his own enquiries because in fact he cannot rely on his subordinate to keep him fully informed. Chief Inspector Heat has his own concept of loyalty, and his own understanding of what his boss needs to know; and The Secret Agent is a beautiful illustration of the need for any director not to take too much on trust, and to find out what is really going on. Readers who are inspired to read the full text will find the two discussions between the AC and the Home Secretary of especial interest in the management of information as an aspect of leadership.

☐ Which aspects of his work does the Assistant Commissioner enjoy, and what does he find frustrating? What should he do about it?

CHAPTER 4

The AC enjoys police work, or more particuarly, detective work, and is frustrated that he has been promoted to a position where he can no longer exercise his practical skills. Consequently, and to their irritation, he practises those skills on his subordinates.

He might have recognised that as a senior manager he would be unlikely to use his detective skills in investigating and solving crimes by his own efforts, and either have resisted promotion or found a new stimulus in mastering the management skills appropriate to his more senior position.

He is lucky in that, given the special nature of CID work, he can at least sometimes justfy his instinct to absorb himself in the details of a case. The AC does not question the process of police work itself, nor find fault with his subordinate, Chief Inspector Heat, for failing to keep him fully informed: he simply finds a way around that problem. We might also comment that he appears to have made the wrong marriage: but he is far from unique in that characteristic!

> ☐ To what extent does power rest upon the manipulation of information? Is this axiom unique to the security services, or does it also apply elsewhere?

The main purpose of the police unit at the heart of this story is to gather and use information in order to protect national security. It is therefore of necessity a secretive bureaucracy in which power derives from the manipulation of information.

Does this maxim apply to other sorts of organisations? Not necessarily. A theatrical company, for example, produces plays, and judges its success by the quality of its productions, the number of people who attend performances, and the profits made. There may be within the company information that is kept secret, or rather, confidential; but we would not judge the manipulation of that information to be a central issue.

By contrast, and if we wished to be paradoxical, we might consider the (successful playwright) George Bernard Shaw's maxim that 'every profession is a conspiracy against the public.' What did he mean by this? An illustration of what he may have had in mind is the instinct to monopoly of the medical profession. A cynic might argue that doctors create and enforce a monopoly for the treatment of medicine, not in the interests of the sick, but so that they may exclude non-qualified but competent practitioners from the business of curing them, and thus charge higher fees for themselves. The key point here is that one of the ways in which professions regulate and exclude is by the creation of a special language, to which only they are privy: and what is that, but the manipulation of information[1]?

A final comment on this subject, on which so much more might be offered, is that it may be the practitioners themselves who are most aware of the pitfalls and dangers of their occupation. Thus, in The Secret Agent, the AC comments to his superior, the Home Secretary, that spies and secret agents cannot be trusted and that their usage gives rise to all sorts of problems. However, to comment on the morality of this would be akin in irrelevance to commenting on the morality of chess.

> ☐ It was stated in the text that life without the occasional lie or other act of deception would be very difficult to sustain (whether at home or at work). What are your views on this? Is lying always wrong, no matter what the motives of the liar, or the demands of the situation? Have you ever been asked, at work, for information that you did not feel entitled to reveal, and if, so, how did you deal with the situation? Is a leader ever entitled to lie or practise deception, and if so, when and how?

There are a number of separate questions that need to be disentangled here. Rather than attempt a short programme in moral philosophy, we shall simply offer some general comments from the perspective of the reasonable person.

---

1   Please see Orwell's comments on Newspeak, elsewhere in this volume. The creation of Newspeak was intended to make Thoughtcrime impossible, since it could not be conceptualised.

1. It is sensible to distinguish between different forms of deception, although the difference may not always be significant. Thus, it may be useful to distinguish between what we might call active and passive deception, or lying by commission and lying by omission; and there is a general assumption that to set out to deceive someone is perhaps more reprehensible (if blame applies) than simply failing to inform that other person of something that he ought to know.

Thus, consider a used car salesman, A, who is interacting with a potential customer, B, over a car, C. Leaving aside his legal obligations, which would be the worse moral position for A?

- A tells B that the car has an excellent safety record, when he knows that it does not; or

- A fails to inform B of the safety record of the car at all.

We suggest that although the result may be the same (the car crashes and B suffers), the first option indicates a worse moral position, in that A has actively chosen to deceive B and to put him and others at risk, in clear breach of his moral (and legal) obligations.

Consider, by contrast, the so-called 'white lie,' and the possible justification for diplomacy rather than either deliberate deception or compulsive honesty. Suppose that A and B, husband and wife, are in a dress shop, and the wife says to the husband:

'How do I look in this dress?' And, almost at the same moment: 'You don't think it makes my bottom look too big?'

We suggest that there is no universally right answers to these questions, and that much must depend on the relationship between husband and wife. However, we may say that a compulsively honest approach is not necessarily right one, and tact and diplomacy may be more appropriate—although sincerity may be challenged.

2. An obligation to respect confidentiality may compel A not to tell B something, which B believes that he has a right to know (assuming, of course, that he has an inkling of the existence of the information in the first place.)

Thus, for example, a factory employee confronts his manager as follows.

'I hear that we're going to close down in six months. Is this true, or not? I need to know. I've got a wife and family, for God's sake!'

The rumour is true; but the manager is under an obligation to respect confidentiality, and there are other interests at stake as well as those of one employee.

How should he deal with this situation? Rather than offer a categorical answer, we would solicit the views of the group towards such a dilemma, and try and tease out the moral assumptions on which they are based, and the practical wisdom that they offer.

3. A manager or leader may believe that he is entitled to deceive his work force, team or unit for a benign end, where to have shared his true feelings *before* the event would have had a counter-productive effect. In such cases, we would suggest that there should be a sharing of the truth as soon as the deception is no longer needed.

We may conclude that the morality of deception is a rich and indeed an almost inexhaustible subject, in which the quality of the discussion is a worthy outcome in itself.

☐ Conrad describes Chief Inspector Heat as not truly wise, in that he allows himself to give an assurance (that no terrorist outrage is about to occur in London) which is very soon falsified by events. On the other hand, Heat has been concerned to project an image of himself as both knowledgeable and confident of his own abilities: a reliable person who deserves his position. He should not have made an assurance that he could not guarantee; but we may understand why he did so.

CHAPTER 4

> Have you ever been asked to provide an assurance when you did not feel fully confident or competent to do so, and if so, how did you deal with the situation?

A wise leader is able to project confidence without giving false promises. Leadership is not a popularity contest, and the leader should avoid the temptation of telling his listeners what they want to hear, for the short-term advantage that he gains thereby.

> ☐ Do you feel that it is the task of the leader to raise the moral tone, as it were, and to refer to grand moral principles as applying to the everyday work of the organisation? Or is it better to operate in the world of *realpolitik*, to accept human nature for what it is, and to seek for pragmatic solutions to practical difficulties as they arise?

This question might be paraphrased, are you a manager or a leader? The task of the manager is surely to seek for pragmatic solutions to practical difficulties, whereas a leader may be expected to raise the moral tone, and to make sure that followers understand and apply the ethical principles that should underly their work. The leadership theorist James MacGregor Burns (Burns, 1978) distinguished between what he called transformational and transactional leadership. A transactional leader bargains with his followers, whereas a transformational leader raises their awareness of what it is possible to achieve. This is similar to the distinction between management and leadership which we may find articulated in other texts, although Burns is perhaps unusual in making the moral aspects of leadership so explicit.

As to what a leader should do, we must leave that to the decision of the reader and the results of any group discussion of this and other questions. (We would, however, support any suggestion, on the whole, that addresses the reality of leadership, and says that leaders sometimes need a little bit of this, and sometimes a little bit of that: not a very scientific formula, perhaps, but one that certainly has its uses!)

Leaders may help to raise or clarify the moral issues that underly at least some of the decisions facing the groups whom they lead, whether formally or informally. However, we would suggest that moral exhortation is not always either necessary or productive, and that to lead by example may be more efficacious. In any case, and whatever is the message that the leader is trying to get across, it should be put in words (which may include images or parables) which his followers can grasp.

Notes

1. I am much indebted to Dr Keith Carabine of the University of Kent, chairman of the Joseph Conrad Society (UK), for his unstinting help in commenting on this chapter in draft form. He is a true scholar and does not hoard his knowledge.
2. Although Conrad does not say so, it is clear that it is the Russian Embassy that employs Verloc.
3. This means that he may be returned to prison at any stage, if the authorities have reason to suspect hat he has retuned to crime.
4. In this novel, Conrad dwells on obesity to a remarkable extent. Michaelis, as we have just read, is remarkably fat, and Verloc is immense, if of a more solid build. His Russian handler, Mr Vladimir, is plump; and Chief Inspector Heat's face is marred by 'too much flesh.' By contrast, Yundt, although physically repulsive, is not overweight, and the Professor is scrawny and physically insignificant. The Assistant Commissioner is described as lean, but sounds far from handsome, as his face has been yellowed by jaundice. Why does Conrad emphasize the obesity or ugliness of his characters, in a way that is not reflected in his other works? We believe that it has something to do with his intentions in writing this 'modernist' novel, in which there are no heroes, and anarchists, police officers and politicians alike are presented as unworthy of admiration.
5. The pamphlets are published by a secret society which calls itself The Future of the Proletariat, which in reality consists of nothing more than four or five anarchists, and is probably funded by the regimes it seeks to destroy, such as Tsarist Russia. Conrad the man was intensely cynical about secret societies, and that contempt is revealed by Conrad the novelist. The title 'The future of the proletariat' contains a delicious irony within itself. If the proletariat is to have a future, it would be most unwise to entrust any part of it to Messrs Ossipon, Yundt and company.
6. The Penguin Classic Edition of *The Secret Agent* refers to the creation of the Criminal Investigation Branch (later department) in 1842. The Special Irish Branch of the Metropolitan Police Service was set up in 1886, specifically to deal with Fenian outrages; and later went on to become the Special Branch, which dealt with all political crimes. The security service, first known as MI5, was set up in 1909 to counter German espionage. See *Police and Policing* (Villiers, 2009.)
7. Conrad goes on to point out that 'a given anarchist may be watched inch

CHAPTER 4

    by inch and minute by minute, but a moment always comes when somehow all sight and touch of him, are lost for a few hours, during which something deplorable (usually an explosion) does happen.' (page 68) It is because of passages like these that John Gray calls him 'Conrad, Our Contemporary.' (Gray, 2004.)

8. Joseph Conrad was to prove a strong influence upon the writer, Graham Greene, and Greene's novel *It's a Battlefield* (1931) contains a lugubrious Assistant Commissioner (also unnamed) who bears a remarkable resemblance to Conrad's original creation.
9. Please see Sylvia Bok's two books (Bok, 1978 and Bok, 1986) for an insightful analysis of the validity of lying in public life, *inter alia*.
10. Conrad claimed that the portrayal of the anarchists in *The Secret Agent* was not intended to be an accurate depiction of such people. Nevertheless, he was wholly pessimistic about revolutionary idealism, which he attacks in a later novel, *Under Western Eyes* — a portrayal of anti-Tsarist Russian terrorists in exile in Geneva.
11. When the author of this text worked as a tutor at the national police staff college, a future chief constable remarked to him that the essential and recurring challenge to the police lay in deciding whom to support, and whom to control. It would seem that the Assistant Commissioner is applying this maxim to good effect; and that it has a wider application than simply to policing.

CHAPTER 5

When the clock strikes thirteen: George Orwell

George Orwell was born in 1903 in India, where his father worked for the opium department of the civil service. His real name was Eric Blair, and he was to keep this name until he became better known as the novelist and journalist who wrote under the name of George Orwell. The reason for his change of name is part of the key to his character. He was, he wrote, appalled by the Norseness of Eric and the Scottishness of Blair. He chose George as a wholly English name, and Orwell after the river in Suffolk. Orwell, despite the gritty realism of most of his writing, was a romantic.

Blair was taken to England by his mother in 1904, and did not see his father again until he was twelve years old. He won a scholarship to preparatory school, which he hated, and then another to Eton, where he appeared to fit in well enough and made lifelong friends, although by character he was both argumentative and happy in his own company. When he left Eton in 1921 he did not go to university, since his father, who had retired on a pension, claimed that he could not afford to pay for his only son to become an undergraduate. Moreover, the young Eric Blair had not done enough work at Eton to win a university scholarship. Instead, this intense, bookish, lonely young man joined the Indian Imperial Police, to be stationed in Burma for five years. This was an understandable choice of career for a young, lower upper middle class Englishman (the description is Orwell's own) who was fascinated by the romance of the East, and like another writer-to-be, Joseph Conrad, felt that he had to go there; but it was a bad choice of career for Eric Blair.[1]

In Burma the young imperial police officer's ideas began to change. Orwell wrote about his Burmese experiences both in his memoirs and in his early fiction, in which the author's views are easily discerned. It would seem that he did not like Burma, and he was all too well aware that the Burmese did not like him. Ideologically, he came to perceive

CHAPTER 5

colonialism as wrong, to dislike his role as an imperial police officer, and to understand and accept the ambitions of the young priests who were the advocates of the end of imperial rule.

At the same time, there were other forces at work. It seems clear that Orwell took his duties as a trainee-superintendent of police conscientiously, and did not attempt to shirk or avoid them. He found the work of a police officer both repetitious and tedious, with no intellectual stimulus other than that of learning Burmese, a task which he took seriously. He found little stimulus in the company of his fellow-expatriates, whose interests, at least as portrayed in his novel *Burmese Days* (published in 1934) were limited to sport, alcohol and adultery, and who had no doubts at all about the proper place of the 'native' in colonial society.

It takes a certain sort of person to be a successful police officer, whether in the imperial police service or not: and it is clear that Orwell was not that sort of person. He had a strong imagination; he was an idealist; he sympathised with the underdog; and he took things to heart. Those are not, in themselves, disqualifications for a life in the police service: but they do not make that choice of career an easier one.

Before we make him out to be a saint, however, we must recognise that there was a strong element of the public school prefect in Orwell's personality. Whilst he may have believed in liberty, his instinct was at least on some occasions towards the exercise of authority. If the radical young Burmese priests did not care for him, he did not care very much for them; he found them sly and underhand and disliked their deceptions. He was, after all, a police officer and a pillar of the Raj which they wished to abolish, and whilst he was a police officer he did his duty.

His feelings about imperialism were summed up in his famous story, *Shooting an Elephant*, from which we quote.

> In Moulmein, in lower Burma, I was hated by large numbers of people – the only time in my life that I have been important enough for this to happen to me. I was sub-divisional police officer of the town, and in an aimless, petty kind of way anti-European feeling was very bitter...

As a police officer I was an obvious target and was baited whenever it seemed safe to do so. When a nimble Burman tripped me up on the football field and the referee (another Burman) looked the other way, the crowd yelled with hideous laughter...

The young Buddhist priests were the worst of all. There were several thousands of them in the town and none of them seemed to have anything to do except stand on street corners and jeer at Europeans.

All this was perplexing and upsetting. For at that time I had already made up my mind that imperialism was an evil thing and the sooner I chucked up my job and got out of it the better. Theoretically – and secretly, of course – I was all for the Burmese and all against their oppressors, the British. As for the job I was doing, I hated it more bitterly than I can perhaps make clear. In a job like that you see the dirty work of Empire at close quarters. The wretched prisoners huddling in the stinking cages of the lock-ups, the grey, cowed faces of the long-term convicts, the scarred buttocks of the men who had been flogged with bamboos – all these oppressed me with an intolerable sense of guilt...

With one part of my mind I thought of the British Raj as an unbreakable tyranny, as something clamped down upon the will of prostrate peoples; with another part I thought that the greatest joy in the world would be to drive a bayonet into a Buddhist priest's guts. Feelings like these are the normal by-products of imperialism; ask any Anglo-Indian official, if you can catch him off duty.

Shooting an Elephant, which is based on his own experience, illustrates the complexity of his personality and the sensitivity of his perceptions. He begins with a typically Orwellian paradox, and goes on to suggest that the only reason why he is compelled to shoot the elephant, which is not trampling people and property underfoot but peacefully feeding, is that the crowd expects it of him. He is the symbol of authority and the font of power: and he must use that power or the crowd will no longer believe in him and the system he represents. In his words, he does not wish to look a fool.

Orwell found that he was unsuited to the work and life-style of an imperial police officer and was able to retire from the service in 1927 on medical grounds. At the age of 24, he found himself unemployed; unqualified for any profession; still dependent upon his family for financial and emotional support; and in every sense of the word, at a loose end.

By the time that Orwell went to Spain in 1936, he had explored the underside of life and had achieved some success as a writer. His path had been a strange one for an Old Etonian and ex-imperial police officer to follow, and was inspired at least in part by a sense of guilt. It seems clear that Orwell did not seek happiness, in any conventional way. Indeed, he went out of his way to avoid it. He had tramped. He had been down and out in Paris and London. He had worked as a kitchen hand, teacher, book-shop assistant, shop-keeper and investigative journalist. His book on the condition of the working class, *'The Road to Wigan Pier'* had made an impact that had eluded the novels he published during this period, although they had not been ignored[2]. He had begun to embrace democratic socialism, but had not estranged himself from his conservatively inclined family. He was educating himself, in his own terms: for despite having been a scholar at Eton he regarded himself as ill-educated. He was refining his views and finding his voice. Perhaps most importantly for his own happiness, this shy, awkward, lonely bachelor had found a wife.

Orwell's experience of any sort of formal leadership after Burma was limited. Nevertheless his work, and especially his 'fairy tale' of *Animal Farm* and his dystopia of *Nineteen Eighty-Four*, reveal an insight into human nature and the inevitability of the failure of any utopia, which have made both them and their author world-famous and a part of our language. Before he wrote those works, however, Orwell was to experience military service as a volunteer in the Spanish civil war, an experience which was to worsen his health and increase his political insight into the totalitarian tendency of European politics on the eve of the Second World War.

CHAPTER 5

Homage to Catalonia

Orwell went out to Spain to 'cover' the Spanish civil war which began in 1936. When he arrived in Spain and saw what was happening for himself, he joined up, as it seemed the obvious and natural thing to do[3]. He joined the anarchist militia or POUM because it was affiliated to the International Labour Party, and he was more sympathetic to the anarchist way of doing things than the autocratic plans of the communists; and he found military service extremely difficult. He was no longer a young man. He suffered acutely from the cold. He was far taller than the average Spanish volunteer, and no Spanish boots or uniform could be found to fit him. He found the militia full of enthusiasm but profoundly undisciplined and was appalled by their casualness with fire-arms. Part of him, the part of him that had been educated at Eton, had served in the Officer Training Corps, and had been trained as an imperial police officer in Burma, must have longed for a more efficient organisation. The stronger part admired the anarchist approach to life and believed that it could be made to work on the battlefield, although he still saw the need for competent generalship.

In the anarchist militia which he had joined, Orwell's military experience, such as it was, and more likely his character and maturity, meant that he served as a corporal in charge of a section of volunteers, and later become a lieutenant. He was a safe pair of hands.

War is dangerous even when not very much is going on, and Orwell's service in Spain came to an abrupt end. He was shot through the neck, and almost killed; and the POUM itself came under attack from its supposed allies on the Republican side in Spain, in a struggle for power. He and his wife Eileen had to flee Spain before he was captured and shot by the communists. By 1938, a disabled Orwell was back in England. During the Second World War he served in the Home Guard and worked for the BBC. By 1945, his wife had died; he was chronically ill; he had an adopted son to bring up on his own; and he was to go and live on a remote Scottish island called Jura which was the worst possible location for a man in his medical condition.

Orwell, who had been ill, on and off, for much of his life, and who was to treat his own health as an issue of profound indifference, was finally to die of tuberculosis in 1950. Before that date, however, he was to write and publish his two best-known works, which made him an international best-seller, which are still in print, and which have added a new phraseology to the English language. They are *Animal Farm* and *Nineteen Eighty-Four*. Neither is a treatise on leadership as such, but both have a great deal to tell us about that subject. *Animal Farm*, which he calls a fairy story, is a fable or satire, and *Nineteen Eighty-Four* a dystopia. Let us explore them both a little further.

Animal Farm

Animal Farm is a satire on the Russian revolution, which Orwell sees as having begun with admirable ideals, only to have been corrupted by the intrinsic imperfection of human nature.

The animals on Farmer Jones' farm are tired of being exploited by their corrupt and useless master. They revolt against him in a spontaneous uprising and take over the management of the farm for themselves.

At first, and after the initial reaction and invasion of the other farmers has been repulsed, the newly named Animal Farm seems like a sort of earthly paradise. The animals work together in natural harmony and under the tenets of 'Animalism' at least two of the ideals of the French Revolution—Equality and Fraternity—have finally been realised. The first ideal, liberty, is less in demand. The animals wish to be free of oppression, but recognise the need for order and discipline in their lives. They do not wish to be free, in any bourgeois sense. They wish to remain working on the farm, and to make it a successful cooperative enterprise—a task which is potentially within their power.

Gradually, things begin to go wrong. The pigs are the most advanced amongst the animals. (In terms of the analogy, they are the equivalent of the intelligentsia in pre-revolutionary Russia, part of whom went on to become the 'vanguard' of the proletariat, and to direct events after the overthrow of the Tsar and the collapse of the provisional government under Kerensky). The pigs take power on behalf of the other animals, and then purely for themselves. The two top pigs,

Snowball (Trotksy) and Napoleon (Stalin) are always at loggerheads, until Napoleon is able to seize supreme power, to expel his rival, and to impose a reign of terror. (Lenin does not appear in the book, although there is an equivalent of Karl Marx. This is a fairy tale, in Orwell's term, and not an exact parody of Russian history.)

The book ends with Animal Farm under a corrupt dictatorship in which the great majority of animals are no better off than under Farmer Jones, and probably worse. The pigs have made themselves a new master class, and are indistinguishable from their human equivalent, the farmers, who have continued to exploit the animals on either side of Animal Farm, and who are now in alliance with its porcine rulers. Napoleon has seized power because he is cunning, ruthless and utterly self-interested: and because he offers his fellow-pigs the chance to share in his gains at the expense of the other animals.

Animal Farm is an allegory in which the animals become real to us, whilst at the same time exerting a symbolic role. It is thus profoundly shocking that Boxer, the shire horse who is both the strongest and the most hard-working of the animals, should be threatened by Napoleon's ferocious dogs and eventually sold to the knackers; for Boxer, who is unable to learn to read and write and who works himself to death on behalf of the others, represents the long-suffering Russian people.

The importance of propaganda

By contrast with Snowball, Napoleon is no orator, and makes use of his acolyte Squealer to persuade the other animals that whatever Napoleon says is right, and that whatever they believed to be true no longer applies. After Napoleon has expelled Snowball from the farm, and removed the only remaining opportunity of the animals to participate in the management of 'their' farm at their regular Sunday meeting, Squealer is sent to explain the new situation in which 'Comrade' Napoleon has in effect seized total power over them.

> '"Comrades," he said, "I trust every animal here appreciates the sacrifice that Comrade Napoleon has made in taking this extra labour upon himself. Do not imagine, comrade, that leadership is a pleasure! On the contrary, it is a deep and heavy

responsibility. No one believes more firmly than Comrade Napoleon that all animals are equal. He would be only too happy to let you make your decisions for yourselves. But sometimes you might make the wrong decisions, comrades, and then where should we be? Suppose you had decided to follow Snowball with his moonshine of windmills—Snowball, as we now know, who was no better than a criminal?"

"He fought bravely at the Battle of the Cowshed," said somebody.

"Bravery is not enough," said Squealer. "Loyalty and obedience are more important. And as to the Battle of the Cowshed, I believe the time will come when we shall find that Snowball's part in it was much exaggerated. Discipline, comrades, iron discipline! That is the watchword for to-day. One false step, and our enemies would be upon us. Surely, comrades, you do not want Jones back?"

Once again, this argument was unanswerable.'

We may also note that on the new animal farm, Napoleon's will is reinforced by a pack of ferocious dogs who have been trained to see him as their master. The combination of propaganda and fear is invincible, and is later to be reinforced by 'show trials' and executions—events with which we are now all too familiar from the history of the Soviet Union, but of which the general public was less aware when *Animal Farm* was first published.

The abuse of language

Orwell worked in propaganda during the Second World War, and *Animal Farm* demonstrates and satirizes the abuse of language by the ruling elite. It is a savage satire. In *Nineteen Eighty-Four*, Orwell was to take his examination of the practices of totalitarianism much further. But *Animal Farm* already shows us how an elite is able to manipulate information and hence control public opinion by the use of some very simple and effective techniques.

We have already seen how Squealer manipulates the emotions of the animals by lying. His spoken lies are backed up by written texts in which the past is altered to suit the present. The original ideals of animalism had been reduced to seven commandments, which were painted on the wall of the big barn. The final commandments were that no animal shall kill any other animal; and that all animals are equal. The pigs wish to break all seven commandments, but do not whitewash them out altogether. Instead, they secretly alter them to suit their own purposes. Thus, the sixth commandment now says that no animal shall kill another animal *without cause*; and perhaps most famously, the final commandment is rewritten as follows:

All animals are equal, *but some animals are more equal than others.*

Or, as the sheep are re-trained to bleat together:

Four legs good, *two legs better.*

Lessons on leadership

What does *Animal Farm* tell us about leadership? In one sense, it is a profoundly depressing message. Political idealism is bound to fail, and any notion of creating a Utopian society on earth will never succeed. Solidarity and fraternity may be very motivating ideals for the have-nots, but cannot withstand the will to power which is the fundamental force in human nature. Napoleon (Stalin) comes to power and remains there because he is able to manipulate his followers by a mixture of deception, propaganda and brutality; and this is in some sense natural. We may note that Orwell never explores Napoleon's motivation or seeks to explain his behaviour by reference to a deprived upbringing, as if Napoleon were in some sense damaged goods, and it were a tragic accident or twist of fate that he had come to power. Napoleon succeeds because ruthlessness will always succeed, and any attempt at the achievement of real communism as envisaged by Marx is bound to fail. Napoleon's motivation is self-evident, effective and rational. The idealistic Snowball, who believes in persuasion and practises leadership by example, cannot stand up against his opponent's will

CHAPTER 5

to power is easily defeated. This is especially as Napoleon's closest followers have trained a pack of ferocious dogs to enforce his will—a logical consequence of his political views.

Napoleon differs from some dictators, not in that he is a pig but because he wants his followers to believe in his *right* to lead. He can only achieve such a reputation by deception, for he is not a natural leader and his real personality is far from charismatic. That personality, however, is irrelevant, for a false personality is built up around him that rests upon a rewritten history and a perverted ideology. On Animal Farm, or rather in Soviet Russia, language itself has become an instrument of deception; and there seems no reason why Napoleon should not remain in power forever.

However, if Orwell paints a blackly depressing picture of the death of utopia, he does at least give us some notion of what it might have been like. Before the pigs come to take all power in Animal Farm, there is a real sense of what it would be like to live in a society which has put into practice the ideals of equality and fraternity, and whose citizens work together for the common good; and Snowball is presented as the lost leader who might have saved the Soviet Union from Stalin's brutal dictatorship.

Any analogy breaks down if taken too far, and we are not entitled to infer from *Animal Farm* that George Orwell was a Trotskyist, or that he believed that Trotsky should have become dictator in place of Stalin. Orwell's political views were firmly based in democratic socialism, and his enemy was totalitarianism of any kind. He believed in something which it is difficult to cast in ideological terms: human decency.

This was the society which Orwell glimpsed in Republican Barcelona, and which he was so much to admire: a society in which class distinctions had been abolished, even to the extent of the use of the familiar 'tu' rather than the formal and distancing 'usted' in conversation between strangers. It was a society which was not to last; but it made an impact. We may find the utopian society in the writings of other idealists; but it was Orwell who described its incarnation and pointed to the pathos of its fragility, both in *Homage to Catalonia* and by analogy in *Animal Farm*.

Nineteen Eighty-Four

Nineteen Eighty-Four presents a horrendous dystopia in which the message is never relieved by any indication of hope. The main character of the book, Winston Smith, is a minor functionary in a totalitarian bureaucracy set in a future Britain which has been re-named Airstrip One. His task is to correct the past in order to show that the present is the result of the smooth and steady progress of the state towards its ideal form as represented by Big Brother, and his society has the means to enable him to do so.

This book takes forward some of what has already been explored in *Animal Farm*, and applies it to human society on a global basis. The world of 1984 has been divided into three competing power-blocks, two of which are always at war. Winston Smith lives in Oceania, which is (apparently) ruled by Big Brother—a dictator who is never actually seen, and whose will is interpreted and enforced by the (Inner) Party. Although Winston is a member of the (Outer) Party, he has neither privileges nor power, and his daily life is one of unrelieved misery, conspicuous for its shortages, drabness, monotony, and compulsory catharsis by means of the 'Two Minute Hate'. All party members are subject to the all-seeing surveillance of the telescreen, behind which lurks the unseen but all powerful Thought Police; and, as in Nazi Germany or Soviet Russia, children are encouraged to spy and inform on their parents. Love does not exist, except for the love of Big Brother; and sex will eventually be eliminated.

Winston is the last of the older generation, who can still vaguely remember a time when Big Brother was not in charge. Younger members of the society cannot do so; and if they did, by some extraordinary fluke, wish to question what was going on, or to speculate about the possibility of alternative political arrangements, they will soon be unable to do so: for the state is altering language itself so that the expression of alternative views will become linguistically impossible. English is being replaced by Newspeak, a drastically simplified language which allows of no modification. Once Newspeak has triumphed, any form of alternative thinking will be impossible, for thoughts cannot be expressed without words. (Music and art, as alternative forms of expression, can simply be taken over altogether by the state and used to manipulate the masses.)

Winston rebels against this situation and secretly keeps a diary, out of the view of his telescreen, in which he can express his own thoughts in his own words—a task which at first he finds impossible. He finds a kindred spirit, Julia—in fact, it would be more accurate to say that she finds him—and they have an affair. She is more cynical than Winston, and believes that everything is manipulated; she does not believe, for example, that there is any real war going on, but that it is a master exercise in media control, designed to appeal to the elemental patriotism of the proles who form the great majority of the population, and keep them from dreaming of freedom. There is no possibility of escape from Big Brother, and bourgeois freedom means nothing. People must survive and seize their happiness where they can.

The affair is clearly doomed. When they choose, the thought police, who have known about the affair all along, arrest them and torture them horribly until both betray each other. The system has succeeded, and Winston has been subjugated into giving up any dream of independence of thought. The last four words of the book are these:

'He loved Big Brother.'

Analysis

Animal Farm points to the failure of revolutionary idealism in the past, and *Nineteen Eighty-Four* points to the impossibility of the creation of an ideal society in the future. In place of any utopia, or indeed a decent and humane society, even if far from perfect, we shall have dystopia. Is that future inevitable? Did Orwell believe that the world was bound to develop as he had indicated, and that there was no possibility of avoiding it? Or was his nightmarish vision intended as a dreadful warning: take action now, before it is too late? And if so, has the danger of which he warned us, passed—or has it simply adopted another form?

CHAPTER 5

Nineteen Eighty-Four is not a perfect novel, in the sense that it achieves a perfect internal coherence. Orwell wrote it on the bleak island of Jura, after his wife had died and he himself was dying of tuberculosis, and he had no time to revise the text he was determined to finish. Some aspects of his dystopia are more puzzling than others, but have an internal logic. O'Brien, for example, the member of the inner party who tortures Winston Smith almost to death, is not presented as a sadist but as someone who believes in what he is doing: but what he is doing to is to make a minor functionary conform to the ideology of doublethink. Rationally, there is no sense in this: why should it matter what Winston Smith believes, as long as he conforms?

As Orwell, saw, it does matter to any totalitarian regime, which is in reality a surprisingly fragile institution that cannot tolerate dissent even in thought. The Soviet Union and its satellite states in the Warsaw Pact sought to ensure not only obedience but total control; and one of the ways they did so was to manipulate the intelligentsia.

The Stasi or secret police of the German Democratic Republic, exercised a Teutonic efficiency to keep so many files that the majority of the population must have been under surveillance, or at least the object of official suspicion, at one time or another: and the GDR devoted huge resources, not to keeping its enemies out, but to keeping its own citizens in. Economically, such policies made no sense; but totalitarian states are not run according to the tenets of economic rationality.

Nineteen Eighty-Four is a salutary warning, and its exploration of Newspeak remains relevant in a world in which freedom of thought and expression remains under attack, despite its supposed protection under human rights law—which does not recognise freedom of thought and expression as an absolute right. Indeed, it is arguable that there are forms of both censorship and self-censorship in contemporary society that Orwell would have identified as unhealthy in a functioning democracy; but to explore such questions is not the primary purpose of this book. In our view, *Nineteen Eighty-Four* does not have very much more to tell us about *leadership* than *Animal Farm*, which we believe to be Orwell's classic.

CHAPTER 5

George Orwell: A reflection

Part of the paradox of George Orwell is that he was almost too successful. His early novels were not a great success, and perhaps did not deserve to be: he was a better journalist and essayist than a novelist. However, his two last works, *Animal Farm* and *Nineteen Eighty-Four* (an extended allegory and a work of science fiction) sold by the million and are still selling to-day, and deserve the global recognition they have achieved. (According to a recent biography of George Orwell, by Jeffrey Meyers, they have sold 40 million copies and have been translated into sixty languages. Naturally, both were officially banned in the Soviet Union—and no doubt read by the O'Briens of the inner party.)

Popular success is not a crime, although some literary critics might almost be presumed to think so; and the huge readership of Orwell's most famous works shows that he was able to reach the mass audience he intended to educate and influence. By writing and eventually publishing *Animal Farm*, he was able to attack the practice of communism in Soviet Russia as a murderous charade, and to expose the roots of that gigantic deception. This was a necessary task, for when Orwell wrote *Animal Farm* in 1944, the Anglo-American literary and intellectual world was still inclined to give a considerable credence not only to the ideals of communism, but to its supposed practice in the Soviet Union.

The public at large, meanwhile, which might have been more sceptical, had been encouraged to regard 'Uncle Joe' with favour as an ally in the war with Nazi Germany. Whatever the real feelings of conservatives such as Winston Churchill towards the Russian dictator, they did not broadcast them during a war in which our enemy's enemy was our friend. Orwell, who had been condemned to death by Russian communists because he had fought with the anarchists in the Spanish Civil War, did not hide his real views. He was determined to expose the reality of any totalitarian regime, be it communist or fascist, and past, present or future.

Orwell had seen contemporary dictatorship at work, and knew its destructive powers. Those powers could be used to destroy supporters as well as opponents, for in a world of shifting truths, no-one could be sure of how to navigate safely. Intellectuals, in his view, were as gullible as anyone else. One of the more pathetic persons in *Nineteen Eighty-Four* is Syme, the analytically-minded dictionary reformer, who despite his whole-hearted support for the Party and its aims is himself liquidated—presumably because his very enthusiasm is a threat.[4] In the brave new world of Airstrip One, no-one is safe against the arbitrary powers of the state, and thought-crime is a charge against which there is no defence.

Orwell and surveillance

If Orwell has succeeded in his intention of warning us of the dangers of totalitarianism, why we say that Orwell's work might almost be considered *too* successful? The answer is a subtle one. Orwell has offered us an instantly memorable phraseology. To describe something as 'Orwellian' may send an agreeable sensation of horror down our spine; but, as the Russian psychologist Pavlov showed in his experiments on animal behaviour, prolonged and repeated exposure to a stimulus diminishes the response. Familiarity breeds not so much contempt, as acceptance; and in our cynical, undiscriminating, 'post-modern' world, in which the worst crime is to be serious and entertainment comes before everything else, Orwell's dystopian vision has found a place that he would not have expected: on the television game Big Brother.

Meanwhile, normal citizens are subjected to involuntary surveillance, as the telescreen of *Nineteen Eighty-Four* has been supplanted by other means. CCTV is used to monitor the ordinary citizen's behaviour on the streets, and his movements from place to place. At the same time, his e-mails, texts, and the dates, times and locations of his mobile telephone calls are automatically recorded and stored by the state, to remain accessible to interrogation (the word is significant) for seven years.

All this is passive 'data', which will not necessarily be processed; but it is of potential use to the state. It is necessary, it is argued, in order to prevent both major and minor crime (or at least, to be more easily

CHAPTER 5

able to investigate it once it has occurred); and the ordinary citizen will surely see no problem with the theoretical loss of liberty that is its consequence.

The argument that the state needs greater powers in order to combat terrorism has gained enormously in strength after 9/11. The so-called 'war on terrorism' (based in Eurasia) justifies almost any counter-measure, including the destruction of the civil liberties that that 'war' is intended to protect. As Squealer might have said:

Surely, Comrades, you do not want Osama bin Laden back?

We are waxing polemical, and that is not the purpose of this book. We do not live in a dystopia, and many of Orwell's imaginings have not come to pass (at least as far as Airstrip One is concerned). Nazi Germany is long dead, as are Fascist Italy and Imperial Japan. The Soviet Union has been consigned to Trotsky's dustbin of history, and if we have not reached the permanent age of democratic capitalism that Santayana recognised with such enthusiasm, some of its enemies are clearly extinct. If the most pressing conflict in the world is now between militant 'Islamism' and what is called 'The West', then there is something almost reassuringly traditional about a confrontation that goes back to the Crusades; even if the so-called 'weapons of mass destruction' may be a more recent development.

But in so far as the state is attempting to control our thoughts, for whatever reason, then Orwell's fears still apply. The United Kingdom is a multi-racial and multi-ethnic society in which the school-leaver Eric Blair could have become the equivalent of an imperial policeman without travelling to Burma to do so. In this globally sensitive environment, racial and ethnic issues are not always freely discussed, for fear of casing offence to a minority, or promoting racial tension. The police have been given extraordinary powers to prosecute 'racially aggravated offences': well-intended legislation which imposes an additional burden on their judgement. Are these developments an unfettered benefit? Not necessarily. As John Stuart Mill wrote in his classic work 'On Liberty', it is only from open debate that ideas are explored and clarified—for those who advocate them as well as for their opponents. Censorship is censorship, whatever its motivation;

and the strongest form of censorship is to censor oneself. If Orwell were able to view contemporary society, he might suggest that totalitarianism is not dead: it has simply assumed different forms.

Questions for reflection

- ☐ Orwell is a master analyst of the role of propaganda, and its importance to the leader (imagine Napoleon without Squealer.) Is it the role of the leader to communicate a clear and simple message about the purpose and philosophy of the organisation? How should that message be communicated? Where does communication stop and propaganda begin?

- ☐ Is Orwell unduly pessimistic in his views on leadership and the sort of people who become leaders? Does power corrupt everyone?

Commentary on questions

- ☐ Orwell is a master analyst of the role of propaganda, and its importance to the leader (imagine Napoleon without Squealer.) Is it the role of the leader to communicate a clear and simple message about the purpose and philosophy of the organisation? How should that message be communicated? Where does communication stop and propaganda begin?

We believe that it is a legitimate and necessary part of the role of the leader to communicate a clear and simple message about the purpose of the organisation, and to say something about how it should set out to achieve that purpose. That message will need to be repeated; and such reinforcement is a form of propaganda.

Where Animal Farm goes wrong is not in the use of propaganda as such. It is in that the pigs have taken power, without consent or accountability; that they rule by a combination of bribery, manipulation and terror; and that their use of propaganda is indistinguishable from lying.

Propaganda and censorship tend to go together: and censorship is not always wrong. Under extreme circumstances such as war, the general censorship of information may be necessary. However, there will, or should be, a difference between the way in which a liberal democracy goes about the process of censorship, and the natural instincts of a dictatorship.

The need to know

We would suggest that under a democratic system, it is the regime that must justify the need for censorship or withholding of information, and its need to ram home a fundamental message. Under a dictatorship it is the other way around, and it is the citizen who needs to be able to show (how?) that access to information is needed. These two different interpretations of the need to know arise from the role of the leader and his relationship to his followers. The leader of a democracy, or a democratic organisation, should be able to act as an adult amongst adults: whereas the relationship between dictator and subject, even at its best, is akin to the relationship between adult and child. (Hence Orwell's choice in naming his 1984 dictator Big Brother, and his satirical attack on the development of Newspeak, which restricts freedom of expression by reducing the words in which thought can be expressed—and thus reduces adults to children.)

- ☐ Is Orwell unduly pessimistic in his views on leadership and the sort of people who become leaders? Does power corrupt everyone?

This question calls for a personal response, and must reflect, at least to some extent, whether the respondent is fundamentally optimistic or pessimistic. (We think it safe to say that Orwell is a pessimist: and that it is hard to prove pessimists wrong.) *Animal Farm* is about the failure of the Soviet Union to turn the ideal of communism into practice, and that ideal is presented as having been corrupted by Stalin

(Napoleon), who is concerned only to achieve his own ends. Was this corruption of an ideal, inevitable? Such quasi-historical questions are impossible to answer; but it seems clear that power tends to corrupt, and that the person who is being corrupted may be the last person to be aware of this: or at least, to acknowledge it. Perhaps no-one, no matter how idealistic, should have absolute or unfettered power over any organisation. Liberal democracy, says the Council of Europe, rests upon three safeguards:

- The rule of law;

- Respect for human rights; and

- The practice of democratic pluralism.

Such safeguards work against the abuse of unfettered power, and indeed the enthusiasm of revolutions; and we must conclude by reinforcing our opinion that George Orwell, who as a boy had won a scholarship to Eton and as a young man had served in the Indian Imperial Police, was a practising democratic socialist, who did more than anyone else to warn his readers of the dangers of unfettered utopianism.

Notes

1 Both Conrad and Orwell wrote about the dark side of imperialism from personal experience, Conrad in the Congo and Orwell in Burma.
2 The interested reader will note that Jack London (q.v.) achieved his major fame as a short story writer and a novelist, but also wrote some journalism as well as semi-autobiographical work. His early book 'The Road' is an unvarnished account of his experiences as a 'hobo.' London knew the life of the working-class, and especially the down-and-outs, as Orwell never could; for London had been one of them. Jack London's account of life on the streets of London, where he lived as an unemployed sailor for his research, is a remarkable piece of writing (*The People of the Abyss, 1904*.)
We must add that Orwell never pretended to be what he was not, and never modified his appearance or accent to suit his audience. He was not a would-be proletarian with estuary accent to match, nor a bored aristocrat in search of the bizarre; and his audience had to take him as they found him. Some did not take to him at all.
3 Compare Ernest Hemingway's experience in Spain, also in this volume. Hemingway went and remained in Spain as a journalist, and did not volunteer

CHAPTER 5

for military service. Had he done so, he would not have joined the anarchists, whom he regarded as unprofessional and therefore ineffective as a fighting force. From Hemingway's sojourn in Spain emerged his classic novel of love and leadership intrigue under conditions of guerrilla warfare, *For Whom the Bell Tolls*.

Hemingway is more famous as a novelist than journalist, whereas it could be argued that Orwell's greatest talents were as a reporter and essayist, and in his ability to convey a political message in the shape of a work of fiction. His early novels, in which he was learning his craft as a writer of fiction, and which have no underlying intent, are of limited appeal. *Animal Farm* is a well-written fable, with an immensely powerful political message; it can appeal at a number of levels. *Nineteen Eighty-Four* is intensely readable and contains some memorable characters, but its main impact is as a dystopian vision of the future.

4   Syme's task as a lexicographer is not to record and explain the meaning of words as they have emerged in the natural process whereby human beings communicate with each other, but to reduce their number, so that eventually thought itself will have been restricted by the absence of alternative means for its expression. Can we express thoughts without words? The relationship between thought and language was explored by the Russian psychologist L S Vygotsky in a book of the same name, and his conclusion is that a word is a microcosm of consciousness.

CHAPTER 6

Journey's End?: R C Sherriff

Stanhope

Supposing the worst happened—supposing we were knocked right out. Think of all the chaps who've gone already. It can't be very lonely there—with all those fellows. Sometimes I think it's lonelier here.

Act II, Scene 2

Journey's End was an astonishingly successful play. It was first performed in London in 1928, and went on to be a theatrical phenomenon that was produced all over the world and catapulted its unknown author onto the world stage—a position he found uncomfortable and was glad to relinquish, for he was the opposite of to-day's 'celebrity.'

Its success was astonishing in every sense. It was written by an insurance clerk, R C Sherriff, who had a minor interest in amateur dramatics, and who had served in the trenches in the Great War. He had no ambitions to become a professional playwright, and had begun to write plays simply to support his local rowing club (Sherriff, 1968)[1].

Journey's End, on which he worked for a year in his limited spare time, was rather different to what he had written before. It was, in a sense, his first real play, and he hoped to take it further: but the odds were almost overwhelmingly against him. When he first offered the play to an agency, Curtis Brown, the reaction was supportive but pessimistic. No-one wanted a play about the war, whatever its merits. Moreover, he was a complete unknown, who would attract neither the backers he needed to invest in his play, nor the big names as actors who might induce the potential audience to buy tickets, *if* he were to obtain the initial backing which was in any case needed.

Their reluctance was understandable and made sound commercial sense. *Journey's End* is a simple story, with a single set[2]. There are eleven

CHAPTER 6

men in the cast and no women. There are no great speeches. (Instead, the dialogue is simple and natural, and relies on understatement and quiet humour.) There is no spectacular demonstration of heroism in action—although the company commander does threaten to shoot one of his officers who is showing cowardice, and he means it. There are no set battles. There is no hatred of the Germans, who hardly appear in the story; and the sergeant-major is instinctively kind to a young German prisoner.

> Raleigh (a new officer)
>
> *The Germans are really quite decent, aren't they? I mean, outside the newspapers?*
>
> Osborne (an older officer)
>
> *Yes. (He goes on to illustrate the point.)*

(Act II, Scene 1)

There is almost no discussion of the rights and wrongs of the war which dominates the lives of the cast, but is still seen as an interlude that will eventually be over—if they survive. And there is no happy ending, but rather a tragedy that has been implied from the first scene. Indeed, a bald summary of the plot and style of this play is likely to suggest an exercise in a minor key: Elgar in place of Beethoven. Or, we might suppose, Terence Rattigan's *Separate Tables* in the trenches.

Such an impression would be wholly wrong, as the audience recognised from its very first performance in the West End,[3] where the impact of the play was so powerful that they sat in silence at its end, too stunned to applaud—an omission which was eventually rectified. This is a strong play, with a profound impact; and it has a great deal to tell us about leadership.

CHAPTER 6

The author

R C Sherriff was born in 1896, educated at Kingston Grammar School, and worked as an insurance clerk as his father and grandfather had done before him. He served as an officer in the First World War, during which he was wounded and reached the rank of captain.

His reaction to the war is conveyed with disconcerting honesty in his autobiography:

> 'When the first war came I'd just left school and started work in a London office. I'd been a big shot at school; captain of rowing and cricket, and record holder of long jump in the sports. From that I had become a junior clerk on a high stool, sticking stamps on envelopes... After that last triumphant term at school it was a demoralising come-down....
>
> 'So when the war came it was a merciful, heaven-sent release. I loved the route marches along the country lanes, singing the marching songs with the band ahead of us. I loved the manoeuvres across the downs and guard duty at night, watching the dawn come up before the trees. It was romantic and exhilarating after those miserable days on an office stool. And when it was all over I went up to the office to show myself with the three stars of a captain on my shoulders and a gold wound stripe on my sleeve.
>
> 'There had been bad times in France, but all in all it had been a magnificent and memorable experience, and with my wounds gratuity I bought myself a sculling boat.'
>
> (Sherriff, 1968, page 317.)

After the war Sherriff returned to his work as an insurance adjuster until his success as a playwright enabled him to become a full-time writer—a decision he embarked upon with great trepidation, and with the personal assurance of the chairman of the company that his old job would be kept open for him.

He seems to have been a very modest person, and claimed that he only began to write plays in order to raise money for Kingston Rowing

Club. *Journey's End* was neither his first or last play, but it was by far his greatest success. After it achieved world-wide fame, he wrote other plays and novels and was for a time a successful script-writer in Hollywood—although he much preferred to work at home in England, where he could enjoy the quiet of the garden, the pleasures of the English countryside, and the constant companionship of his mother. He enjoyed an interlude at Oxford University as a very 'mature student' of 34, but did not complete his degree. Sherriff"s second and third plays were commercial failures, but he was eventually able to achieve further success on stage; his last play was an historical study of the Romans in Britain. When theatrical fashion changed with the New Movement in the early 1950s he recognised that his style of play would no longer suit the critics, and laid down his pencil to enjoy his hobbies. He never married, and appears to have been perfectly content with the society of his mother, who accompanied him both to Oxford and Hollywood.

R C Sherriff died in 1975.

Sherriff's place in literature

R C Sherriff is hard to classify. He is best known for one play, which was a phenomenal success: he also published a successful novel. *Journey's End* was lavished with praise by the critics, as well as by leading figures such as Winston Churchill; but in later years the critics turned against Sherriff's final efforts, which were criticised as behind the times and sentimental. Sherriff's work in Hollywood and later for Alexander Korda, the Hungarian-British film producer, won popular acclaim but did not attract the attention of those whom he would have regarded as the high-brows of literature. Perhaps Sherriff was too successful, and earned large sums too easily: they might have preferred him if he were starving in a garret.

When Sherriff met other literary people, he does not seem to have regarded himself as their equal, or even as being engaged in the same occupation. He writes with gentle irony of an almost silent meeting with an intensely shy J M Barrie, the leading playwright of his time and author of *Peter Pan*; and he was so overwhelmed to be invited to visit his childhood literary hero, Rudyard Kipling, that he went to lunch at 'Batemans' and asked the equally reserved poet of empire nothing at all. He preserved the *persona* of the insurance adjuster who had struck lucky; although that persona appears to have been some distance removed from the truth.

Journey's End, like its author, is in some ways equally difficult to classify. It is set in the war, but it is not a war play in the sense that war is its dominant theme. It does not set out to emphasize the pathos and futility of war, as did the war poets Graves, Owen and Sassoon; or their German equivalent, Erich Maria Remarque, in his classic novel, *All Quiet on the Western Front*. It does not laud fighting as a noble preoccupation, as the German soldier turned writer Ernst Junger (1895-1998) was accused of doing in his memoir of the trenches from a storm-trooper's perspective, *Storm of Steel*.[4] Nor is it a wholesale attack on the generals who were accused of unnecessary sacrifice: for although Stanhope feels very bitter about this, it is not a major theme in the play.

> Colonel (who is excited by a raid, and has completely forgotten that there must have been casualties)
>
> *Oh—er—what about the raiding-party? Are they all safely back?*
>
> Stanhope
>
> *Did you expect them to be all safely back, Sir?*
>
> (Act III, Scene 2)

Journey's End: The plot

As with other texts, we shall here offer only enough of the plot or story for our readers to be able to relate to the leadership issues raised, and for them to wish to read the full work for themselves—or in this case to see the play performed on stage.

Journey's End is set in a trench dug-out on the Western Front, and takes place over four days in April 1918. The main characters are the company commander of an infantry company, Captain Stanhope; his second in command, Lieutenant Osborne; and a young subaltern who has just joined the company, Second Lieutenant Raleigh. There are other officers and soldiers in the cast, which is a wholly male one.

Captain Stanhope and his problems

The play deals with the relationship between a damaged company commander and his fellow officers, and in particular his reaction to the arrival of the new officer. This dramatically necessary change to the *status quo* acts as the catalyst to provoke a crisis. Stanhope and Raleigh knew each other before the war, when Stanhope was Raleigh's hero at boarding school. In addition, they knew each other socially, and Stanhope was attracted to Raleigh's sister, although he did not fully realize it at the time.

However, Stanhope has changed enormously from the bright young public school hero who went off to war in 1914. The former sportsman and disciplinarian is now an alcoholic on the verge of a nervous breakdown, keeping going after three years of trench warfare only with the aid of John Barleycorn. He is acutely aware of his own decline, and acutely nervous as to Raleigh's revised opinion of him. How is he to command Raleigh and retain his respect? What is he to do about the unwelcome memories that his arrival provides, and the dreams, hopes and ambitions that he can no longer realize? Osborne does his best to reassure Stanhope, and to prepare the new arrival himself for the change in his former hero: but there is a limit to what he can do.

> Osborne
> *You know, Raleigh, you mustn't expect to find him—quite the same.*
>
> Raleigh
> *Oh?*
>
> Osborne
> *You see, he's been out here a long time. It tells on a man—rather badly—*
>
> Raleigh
> *Yes, I suppose that it does.*
>
> (Act I)

CHAPTER 6

Osborne's background and character

Lieutenant Osborne is an older man known as Uncle who is Stanhope's confidante, besides being his second in command. Stanhope trusts Uncle, who knows both his strengths and weaknesses and is wholly loyal to his company commander.

The play begins with Uncle's loyalties being put to the test. Stanhope's company has replaced another in the front line, and the departing officer in charge, Captain Hardy, is highly critical of Stanhope and asserts that Osborne should be in command—a suggestion that Osborne rejects because he is convinced of Stanhope's superior merits.

> Osborne
>
> *Don't be an ass. He was out here before I joined up. His experience alone makes him worth a dozen men like me.*
>
> Hardy
>
> *You know as well as I do, you ought to be in command.*
>
> Osborne
>
> *There isn't a man to touch him as a commander of men. He'll command the battalion one day if—*
>
> Hardy
>
> *Yes, if! (He laughs)*

(Act I)

Osborne feels deeply sympathetic to his company commander, and counters Hardy's cynical and uncaring attack:

> Hardy
>
> *I mean, after all—Stanhope really is a sort of freak; I mean it is jolly fascinating to see a fellow drink like he does—glass after glass. He didn't go home on his last leave, did he?*
>
> Osborne
>
> *No... Do you know how long he's been out here?*

CHAPTER 6

> Hardy
>
> *A good time, I know.*
>
> (Act I)

Osborne quietly points out that Stanhope has served for nearly three years in the trenches and has never had a break. He is a dedicated and conscientious officer and Osborne would give his life for him. Hardy backs off. His attitude to life is wholly different, and Stanhope is, perhaps, for him a freak in more ways than one.

At some level of consciousness, Osborne may also be aware that he has found the ideal position for himself as the loyal and supportive second in command, who exercises insight, offers advice, and provides the support which his superior needs and without which he could not function.

It is one of the dramatic ironies of the play that we see immediately that Captain Hardy, who criticizes Stanhope so freely, is a poor officer himself, slapdash, selfish and lazy: he does not know anything about his stores, and is not even aware where his men are sleeping.

> Osborne
>
> *Aren't you going to wait and see Stanhope?*
>
> Hardy
>
> *Well, no, I don't specially want to see him. He's so fussy about the trenches. I expect they are rather dirty. He'll talk for hours if he catches me.*
>
> (Act I)

Osborne, however, does not criticise the cheerful Hardy, but merely bids him farewell. They are both serving in the trenches and both face the same dangers; and it is the luck of the draw that Osborne will face the next attack and not Hardy.

CHAPTER 6

Raleigh: the unsuspecting catalyst

Second lieutenant Raleigh is an innocent, naïve and well-meaning young man who is determined to do his best and is delighted to have joined his hero's company: a sentiment that his company commander fails to share. Stanhope does not know how to deal with him, and mistakenly censors his letter home: only to find that the harsh appraisal of himself that he had expected is far from what has actually been written.

Osborne reads out Raleigh's letter to Stanhope, who is pretending to censor it.

> Osborne
>
> *He says: 'And now I come to the great news.* (Raleigh reported to his company and met Osborne in the dugout) *and then later Dennis came in. He looked tired, but that's because he works so frightfully hard, and because of the responsibility. Then I went on duty in the front line, and a sergeant told me all about Dennis. He said that Dennis is the finest officer in the battalion, and the men simply love him. He hardly ever sleeps in the dugout; he's always up in the front line with the men, cheering them on with jokes, and making them keen about things, just like he did at school. I'm awfully proud to think he's my friend.'*
>
> (There is silence. Stanhope has not moved while Osborne has read.) *That's all.* (Pause) *Shall I stick it down?*

(Act II, Scene 1.)

The second psychological crisis of the play, as it were, is when Osborne is killed. Not only does this remove Stanhope's main source of support: it forces him to confront and to censure Raleigh. Firstly, he stares at the shocked young officer, who has just taken part in his first raid:

> Stanhope
>
> *Must you sit on Osborne's bed?*

(Act III, Scene 2)

CHAPTER 6

Secondly, he shouts at him, when Raleigh has failed to join the other officers in a 'celebration' dinner:

Stanhope (shouting)

Are you going to eat your dinner?

Raleigh

Good God! Don't you understand? How can I sit down and eat that when—his voice is nearly breaking—when Osborne's lying—out there—

(Stanhope rises slowly. His eyes are wide and staring: he is fighting for breath, and his words come brokenly)

Stanhope

My God! You bloody little swine! You think I don't care! You think you're the only soul that cares!

Raleigh

And yet you can sit there and drink champagne—and smoke cigars—

Stanhope

The one man I could trust—my best friend—the one man I could talk to as man to man—who understood everything—and you think I don't care—

Raleigh

But how can you when—?

Stanhope

To forget, you little fool—to forget! D'you understand? To forget! You think there's no limit to what a man can bear?

(Act III, Scene 2)

CHAPTER 6

Production

Sherriff, an unknown dramatist who had begun to write plays almost by accident, finished *Journey's End* at an inn in Devon and offered it for production. At first, no theatrical producer could be persuaded to consider it. The Great War was over and no-one wished to revisit its horrors: neither its survivors nor those who were too young to have served. In 1929, eleven years after the conflict ended, Sherriff's play was given an airing in London and a very promising young actor named Laurence Olivier took the part of the company commander, Dennis Stanhope. The production was a triumph, and the play was soon transferred to the West End, where it ran for 595 performances and brought both national and international fame to its author. It remains popular to-day, and is revived on the professional stage from time to time, as well as being produced in amateur dramatics.

Why was this simple and unaffected drama so successful, and what does it have to tell us about leadership?

Success as a drama

In the first place, Journey's End is an outstanding *play*. The setting is entirely gripping, the plot unfolds clearly, and the dialogue is realistic for the time. It contains humour, confrontation and pathos. The characters are convincing, and we could imagine ourselves in their place: we feel sorry for their situation and at the same time admire their capacity to cope. There are no false heroics, and Stanhope is presented as a flawed personality, who has resorted to alcohol under the pressure of trench warfare. He is a good commander, popular with his men, but his character shows great signs of strain.

His relationship with the other officers is explored deftly and in depth, and we are gripped by their common plight as they face the big 'push' that hangs like the sword of Damocles over the entrance to the trench dug-out in which they spend much of their time. Tension builds up as the play progresses, and the use of sound-effects is especially effective. Much of the dialogue has nothing to do with the war, and is all the more poignant as a result. Trotter is concerned with the food, for which the soldier-servant, Mason, is constantly apologising. Osborne reads Lewis Carroll, and discusses rugby football with Raleigh, or the beauty of the sunrise with Stanhope. Stanhope, however, has no means by which to relax, except for oblivion in whisky.

Positive impact

The impact of the play as a whole is positive. It is a tragedy but it does not lead us to despair of human nature. Indeed, the overall message, if there is one, for Sherriff is far too subtle a playwright simply to write a play to convey a message, is one of hope. The tragedy of the Great War cannot be avoided, and war itself is a futile and contradictory activity; but our belief in human nature is strengthened.

Enduring values

Finally, *Journey's End* appeals, I believe, because it presents a portrayal of the English as they would like to be. The officer who represents the values and behaviour of the ideal Englishman is Lieutenant Osborne, whose nickname, 'Uncle', gives the key both to his character and role. Osborne is the second in command of the infantry company, to whose commander he is intensely loyal. His task is to support its officer commanding both in his military duties and by providing emotional support. Osborne, at least for this viewer, is an immensely appealing character. He is older than the other officers, but still active. He is modest, patient, balanced and understanding: he knows himself, and has nothing to prove. We learn that before he volunteered for the war he was a schoolmaster in Hampshire, and had once played rugby for England. Unlike Stanhope, who dare not go home on leave to England and contents himself with the supposed delights of leave in Paris, Osborne is happily married. His patriotism is implicit rather than intrusive and he willingly admits that the football match that took place between the British and German troops at Christmas 1914 does rather indicate the stupidity of war. [5]

CHAPTER 6

Class

From a sociologist's perspective, *Journey's End* might be seen as an analysis of the mores of the officer class which the British public school system had set out to develop, and how that class coped with the pressures of the Great War. The play is constructed from an insider's perspective and the public school system which has educated the main characters in this play is not so much approved as taken for granted. Stanhope, Osborne and Raleigh are all a product of the public school system, but it is Osborne, the older man (and school-master) who has the deeper understanding.

> Osborne
>
> *Small boys at school generally have their heros.*
>
> Stanhope
>
> *Yes. Small boys at school do.*
>
> Osborne
>
> *Often it goes on as long as—*
>
> Stanhope
>
> *As long as the hero's a hero.*
>
> Osborne
>
> *It often goes on all through life.*
>
> (Act I)

This is not the whole discussion of hero-worship, which Uncle perceives as both natural and beneficial if not taken to excess; but the class system which has given the officers very much the same values, outlook and prejudices is taken for granted.

So should it be, for this is a 'real' play about 'real' people and not a sociological analysis. Moreover, a good play shows what people are like by what they do, rather than by what they say. Military service can give rise to the most extraordinary paradoxes; but the purpose of *Journey's End* is not to explore class attitudes to war, but to present a drama which has a universal aspect.

CHAPTER 6

What does the play tell us about leadership?

In our view, *Journey's End* could serve as a master-class in leadership. It indicates, not by exposition but by demonstration, that:

- Leadership is necessary

Stanhope may be a flawed character, but his role is a necessary one. The company needs a commanding officer who must set and maintain standards, lead by example, and act as a focus for the admiration and loyalty of his men. His followers *expect* to be led.

- The leader need not be perfect

Sherriff writes in his autobiography of the sort of man that Stanhope was (for the character had become real to him). He does not refer to him as a public school hero, but as a tough, drink-sodden company commander: the sort of man who was actually to be met in the trenches. He was far from perfect; but he was the sort of commander with whom his men (and later, the audience) could identify.

- 'Charisma' and its vagaries

Leaders are sometimes described as 'larger than life,' or having 'charisma.' We would suggest that 'charisma,' in this vague sense, is neither necessary nor sufficient for leadership, since there have been plenty of successful leaders who did not display it. The charismatic leader is a recognised type, and is conspicuous for his flaws as well as his virtues. Such faults, provided that they have a certain generosity about them, may be part of what makes him admired: and as he proceeds to his third wife, or smashes up an even more expensive motor car, or reels out of the night club at dawn to triumph at the power breakfast or board meeting a few hours later, he is living out in reality what at least some of his admirers have imagined in their dreams.[6]

- Appearance and reality

Arguably, a leader must appear to be what his followers expect. He needs, in other words, to portray the right image. But what is that image? When *Journey's End* was first cast, both director and writer knew exactly what they were looking for in Stanhope; an actor who would come across, not as an accomplished performer, but as ' the real thing;' a real soldier in a real dug-out. The man whom they chose to play Stanhope was called Colin Clive, who was then 29 and may already have acquired the drinking problem which was to contribute to his early death at 37. He was nervous at his audition and read his lines badly. Paradoxically, this worked to his advantage; for Sherriff commented that this was just what Stanhope himself would have done. (The also-ran, Colin Keith-Johnston, was almost too impressive. He had been an infantry officer in the Great War and had won the Military Cross for his valour: but he was somehow less convincing than the stuttering Clive. His substantial compensation prize was to play the part on Broadway.)

- The leader needs support

We have said that the leader must set an example. This presents Stanhope with his greatest difficulty, since his character is an obviously flawed one, and he can no longer play the role of the captain of school that he once offered so convincingly. He can, however, continue to function as a leader if he has support; and he obtains this in abundance, not only from the hero-worshipping Raleigh but his immensely helpful second-in-command, Osborne.

- The leader must confront and overcome doubts and uncertainties: but not necessarily by overt 'heroics'

Stanhope does this in part by shared irony, as when he tells his sergeant-major that they will defeat the enemy in the next 'push' and win the war—a statement that both men know to be untrue.[7] Stanhope is playing the role of the confident leader, but at the same time hinting at his real feelings to the sergeant-major. We may note the significance of the word 'role.' Leadership *is* role-play. A leader is not an actor: but an actor may be a leader, provided that he lives by his script.

- The leader must confront weaknesses in others, even at the price of admitting the same weakness in himself

CHAPTER 6

The weakness once recognised can than, at least in hope, be faced and overcome. This tactic can be a leadership ploy, insincerely practised as a way of manipulating followers; although Stanhope is sincere. Stanhope is more successful in confronting the cowardice in one of his officers, Hibbert, who pretends to neuralgia, than in facing his own inner demons. Stanhope tells Hibbert, as he also confesses to Uncle earlier in the play, that he is sick with fear in the trenches, after what he has experienced over three years; and that Hibbert and he will go out and face the danger together.

Stanhope

We've all got a good fighting chance. I mean to come through — don't you?

Hibbert

Yes. Rather.

(Act II, Scene 2)

The Enigma of R C Sherriff

R C Sherriff remains an enigma, and his autobiography fails to explain the mystery. Indeed, the apparently artless story of his life is as carefully constructed as any work of fiction, and it would appear that he is determined to give little away. The major (and indeed the most interesting) part of the book is devoted to the story of *Journey's End*, rather than its author, about whom very few facts are given.

Sherriff presents himself as an inveterate worrier and a person of what would now be called low self-esteem. He saw himself as an ordinary chap and certainly no intellectual; and he seems to have been reluctant to admit, even to himself, that in *Journey's End* he had created a great play which deserved its success.

As far as he was concerned, the less 'theatrical' the play appeared, the better: and his intention was that the audience share the experience of being in the trenches. Some of his audience had already been there, and may even have looked back upon the war with some nostalgia, for the reaction of the war-poets was atypical. The play is an unstated homage to the courage and decency of the men who lived and died in Flanders, and perhaps to those who survived. E M Remarque dedicates his book, *All Quiet on the Western Front*, to those who, even if they have survived its bombs and bullets, were still destroyed by the war. Sherriff conveys a more positive message.

Personal impact and identification

Any work of art tells us something about ourselves: both how far we are prepared to explore and confront our own background and prejudices, and what value there may be in such an exercise. Others might see this play and identify only the fallacies and false perceptions that it takes for granted: the public school system, the class-differences of English society, the inability to communicate his feelings of the tongue-tied Englishman. But it has shown a universal appeal; and its phenomenal success as a play confirms that it was able to cross all boundaries.

Stages on life's way

What did this play provide for me? Here is my own confession. When I first became aware of this play, I had been though the single sex, boarding-school system, and learned to hero-worship other boys, especially those who were especially athletic or courageous in sport. My first experience of authority, outside the family, was not so much with the masters who taught us as with the older boys who were placed in charge of day-to-day discipline, and whom I either extravagantly worshipped or condemned.[8] Moreover, I still remembered what it was like to be an adolescent. I had wanted to know what I was made of. I had wondered how I would fare in war. I had read the war poems of Siegfried Sassoon, Wilfred Owen, and Robert Graves. I identified with the young subaltern.

The years passed, and I obtained some degree of experience (if not of any real self-knowledge). I became competent in certain areas, and recognised my irredeemable weaknesses in others. Given the necessary courage, I could have been the cynical but still competent company commander. He spoke to me in terms of Kipling's 'If': and even the idea of being drink-sodden had a certain masculine appeal. I liked his approach. Stanhope was tough, unemotional, uncommunicative, and a man with only one real friend. He did not shirk his duty, whatever the cost. I identified with the company commander who lived on the edge, and who, like Conrad's Lord Jim, could not go home again.

Which leaves Uncle, who has reached maturity, and no longer wishes or needs to be the leader; but who is able to provide the emotional support of which the apparent leader is in need. How is he able to do so? Because he *cares*. Uncle knows himself for what he is, and is therefore able to love himself, in a proper way: and it is only Uncle who is really able to love others. Real love is not hero-worship; and it is not blind. It does not stoop to conquer. Uncle has learned to live with himself, and to understand the logic of Christ's fundamental commandment: to love others as we love ourselves requires that we must first be able to love ourselves.

Questions for reflection

- What are Captain Stanhope's strengths and weaknesses, as a human being?

- What are his strengths and weaknesses, as a leader?

- Why does he find it so difficult to deal with the new officer, Second Lieutenant Raleigh?

- How would you describe the character of Lieutenant Osborne?

- Should Lieutenant Osborne be the company commander?

- What did R C Sherriff seek to achieve, in writing this play?

- What are the lessons on leadership conveyed by this play to you, outside the trenches?

CHAPTER 6

Commentary on questions

☐ What are Captain Stanhope's strengths and weaknesses, as a human being?

Dennis Stanhope has extraordinary drive and determination and sets high standards both for himself and others. He is portrayed as the public school hero who is almost always 'on parade,' as it were, and it would be a mistake to judge him by (somewhat caricatured) present day values, for example by suggesting that he finds it difficult to share his feelings, or that he is too strict with another officer who is on the verge of a nervous breakdown. Stanhope is under immense pressure after so long in the trenches, and appears close to breakdown himself; but that is hardly a weakness. Other company commanders would have broken down, or sought relief. Captain Stanhope soldiers on.

☐ What are his strengths and weaknesses, as a leader?

Stanhope is admired by almost everyone as an excellent leader, if an alcoholic. His style of leadership is appropriate for the Western Front in early 1918, and he has earned the respect of both officers and men. His weaknesses as a leader are perhaps the same as his weaknesses as a human being, and relate to the next question.

☐ Why does he find it so difficult to deal with the new officer, Second Lieutenant Raleigh?

Raleigh reminds him of his past, and of the life to which he feels he cannot return. Moreover, Raleigh's sister was his girl; and he is too ashamed of what he feels that he has become, to see her again, or even to wish to think about her. Stanhope has set himself impossible standards, and does not realise that his family and fiancée might judge him less harshly than he judges himself, and show understanding and compassion for what he has become, rather than condemn him out of hand. He cannot face going home.

☐ How would you describe the character of Lieutenant Osborne?

CHAPTER 6

Osborne is a man at peace with himself.

- ☐ Should Lieutenant Osborne be the company commander?

Not in our view, unless to give Stanhope relief in going on leave. Osborne is both happy and effective in playing a supporting role. In a sense, Stanhope's leadership is only effective because of Osborne's loyal support, which is both practical and emotional. As Stanhope says, 'Uncle' is the only man to whom he can talk.

- ☐ What did R C Sherriff seek to achieve, in writing this play?

Here I can only speculate, as his autobiography presents a low-key account. At a practical level, he claimed that he wished to write a successful play that would benefit his rowing club; but I think that this modesty disguised greater ambitions.

Sherriff offered a tribute to the men with whom he had fought in the trenches, so many of whom had died; and he wanted them to be remembered for what they were and not as the creation of a propaganda machine.

Sherriff sought to present trench warfare as it was, and to tell the world what the experience was like; and I think he wanted to tell the world that war had not destroyed the essential humanity of those who fought and suffered and died—and spent much of the rest of their time drying socks and complaining about the food. Like all true artists, he sought to tell the truth; and he succeeded.

- ☐ What are the lessons on leadership conveyed by this play to you, outside the trenches?

Leaders, like other people, need emotional support, under any circumstances, and the relationship between leader and follower or followers is a reciprocal one.

Leaders, like other people, should try to express their emotions as best they can, and not seek solace in alcohol or other artificial and destructive stimulants *because they were unable to do so*. They are human beings, and should not be expected to be perfect (i.e., impervious to emotional or physical stress.)

Leaders, like other people, should seek to know and be at peace with themselves (although this may possibly reduce the drive they bring to their leadership.)

Journey's End is set in war, and might be said to support the virtues of courage, loyalty and fidelity, and to indicate the value of comradeship in adversity. These are enduring qualities, and:

- ☐ Their value is not restricted to the arena of trench warfare in the Great War;

- ☐ They are not the exclusive property of the public school system and its products;

- ☐ They are not restricted to men.

Once more into the breach, dear friends…

It is not, in our view, the task of the leader to address his organisation as if it were at war, when it is not. That is why, amongst other reasons, we did not set out in this volume to exalt the example of leadership portrayed by Henry V at the siege of Harfleur or the Battle of Agincourt, in Shakespeare's play *Henry V*. Oratory has its place, and followers may sometimes need to be inspired to attempt what they did not believe to be possible: but the military metaphor can be a dangerous one.

The importance of duty

Stanhope and his followers do their duty, without shirking, without complaining, and without finding others to blame for their own failings, whether real or perceived. The need for duty did not end on 11 November 1918, and applies to leaders and followers alike. The

CHAPTER 6

interpretation of what constitutes a proper duty, however, imposes a special obligation upon the leader. Leadership cannot be entirely a shared responsibility.

Notes

1. I have used Sherriff's autobiography to provide the background information to the story of his most successful play, as well as to find out something about the man himself. The autobiography is far more informative about the play than its author, who presents himself as an ordinary man who happened to create a theatrical phenomenon. However, there are hints of another person behind that façade.
2. The play has been adapted to other settings, for example in the film *Aces High* (1976) in which the protagonists are fighter pilots on the Western Front, and the action takes place in the air. Additional scenes have been added, including a visit to a brothel; and there is a dinner at which a shot-down German pilot is entertained before being surrendered into official captivity, which suggests that the spirit of chivalry is not wholly dead. The film is well-acted, and is distinguished by a remarkable performance of the role of 'Uncle' by Christopher Plummer. It was directed by Jack Gold and the screenplay was written by Howard Barker. As Sherriff himself would have recognised (for he was to become in later life a screen-writer who specialised in adaptations) it is faithful to the spirit of the original play.
3. *Journey's End* was first given two performances by the Stage Society in London, at the Apollo Theatre. They had recognised the merits of the drama and their production secured critical approval; but such recognition was no guarantee that the play would go any further. A young actor named Laurence Olivier played Captain Stanhope, a role he was later to describe as his most satisfying part. However, he was unavailable to play the same role when the play went on to its extraordinary run at the Savoy Theatre and thence worldwide.
4. Although his works were read with approval by the Nazi leaders, Junger was not a prototype Nazi. *Storm and Steel* contains an episode in which the German storm-troopers break into a British officers' dug-out, to find arm-chairs clustered around an open fire-place. Rather than ridicule his enemy as effete aristocrats, Junger writes of them with a respectful affection: the Anglo-Saxons were a worthy enemy who shared his professional attitude to war, but practised it in their own way. In the same book, he admits to losing his nerve in an unoccupied enemy trench, and going into a blind panic. Leaders need not be invulnerable.
5. We may assume that Osborne is a volunteer rather than a conscript for service in the trenches, for his age and occupation would have prevented his conscription, and he is in any case the sort of quietly patriotic person who would have seen it as his duty to serve. Mass enrollment and then conscription brought a different sort of person (and officer) into what had been a very small, conservative and unquestioning British institution: the peace-time, long-service, British army, which had been essentially unchanged for a very long time

and had only adopted khaki dress when its adoption became an overwhelming imperative during the Boer War.

Conscription brings certain advantages to an army, including a more questioning attitude to its rituals; and can add a welcome element of humour to the prevailing orthodoxy. This phenomenon was not confined to the British army. During the Great War, a large number of Viennese intellectuals were called up to do their bit for the dual monarchy of Austria-Hungary, and the avant-garde composer Arnold Schoenberg was amongst them. We may picture the scene as he described it in his memoirs, on his first parade. The officer surveyed the motley collection of ageing reservists who had been assembled, and asked which of them was the notorious Schoenberg. Silence reigned, since the conscripts had already learned not to volunteer for anything, even to provide information. Finally, Schoenberg stepped forward.

"Beg to report, Sir", he said apologetically, "as no one else is volunteering, that would be me." The reaction of the officer to this truly Austrian confession is not recorded.

6   In that sense, the charismatic leader who lives life to excess is the opposite of Walter Mitty, James Thurber's most memorable fictional creation. Walter Mitty escapes from his miserable, hen-pecked little life into the magnificence of his fantasies of heroism and power. The charismatic leader lives out the fantasies of which his followers can only dream.

7   An American commander at the Battle of the Bulge in 1944 was informed that the Germans surrounded them on all sides. 'Well,' he is reported to have said, 'they can't get away from us now.'

8   My captain of school was called Michael Morpurgo: a confident disciplinarian and natural leader. He joined the army, which would have seemed his manifest destiny—and went on to reinvent himself as a children's writer.

CONCLUSION

All journeys have an end, and I have almost reached mine. What you may have learned on that journey is a matter for you to reflect upon for yourself, as you have already begun to do; and if these selections have encouraged you to read the works quoted from in full, then that is an additional benefit.

Before I conclude the subject of selections, however, I had promised to offer you something on Shakespeare.

Henry V: the strong leader in war

Shakespeare's Henry V is the supreme orator, who invades France on a desperate (but legitimate) mission and rallies his troops at the siege of Harfleur:

> *Once more into the breach, dear friends,*
> *Or close the wall up with our English dead.*
> *In peace, there's nothing so becomes a man*
> *As modest stillness and humility;*
> *But when the blast of war blows in our ears*
> *Then imitate the action of the tiger;*
> *Stiffen the sinews, summon up the blood...*

Before the Battle of Agincourt that follows, Henry takes a different approach. He answers the Earl of Westmoreland, who had wished for more soldiers, by saying that they are already quite enough:

> *We few, we happy few*
> *We band of brothers*
> *For he to-day that sheds his blood with me*
> *Shall be my brother, be he ne'er so vile*
> *This day shall gentle his condition*
> *And gentlemen in England now abed*
> *Shall think themselves accurs'd they were not here*
> *And hold their manhoods cheap whiles any speaks*
> *That fought with us upon Saint Crispin's day...*

CONCLUSION

Henry V is presented as the ideal leader, both by Shakespeare himself and the theatrical offshoot in leadership coaching that has grown up around his works. Laurence Olivier, who cut his theatrical teeth as a 21 years old actor playing Captain Stanhope in *Journey's End*, went on to become the leading actor of his day; and this outstandingly handsome and charismatic star was chosen to play Henry V when the play was filmed in 1942 to raise national morale, not for a conflict in medieval France but with Nazi Germany.

Henry V's great set speeches as a commander are perfect inspirational material for troops facing battle. How might they be best used, in a non-martial setting? Should they be used in other contexts at all? The language of business is already replete with military metaphors: is it time for a change? I leave those questions for the reader to ponder.

Hamlet: A study in delayed reaction?

On the face of it, the play *Hamlet* might almost be seen as an object lesson in how *not* to be a successful leader, for Hamlet is usually criticised for his procrastination rather than for any great display of bold decisiveness. His central mission, as it were, is to avenge his father, but he fails to do so for nearly five acts; and when he finally kills the murderer, his uncle Claudius, it is not the culmination of a considered plan but the result of a twist of circumstances.

Why does Hamlet fascinate us so much; and why is this prolonged study in indecision so full of lessons on leadership? Perhaps we all recognise something of ourselves in Hamlet; and in any case, it is hard not to be seduced by the language. Many people may have felt disillusioned with the human race on occasion, perhaps, but have not expressed their views in these words:

> *What a piece of work is man, how noble in reason,*
> *How infinite in faculties, in form and moving how*
> *Express and admirable, in action how like an angel,*
> *In apprehension how like a god, the beauty of the*
> *World, the paragon of animals—and yet, to me, what is*
> *This quintessence of dust? Man delights not me. No,*
> *Nor woman neither.*

CONCLUSION

Hamlet's character

Hamlet does not so much shirk moral responsibility as wallow in it. Reluctant to accept that he already knows the truth, however, this experimentally minded heir apparent is constantly seeking for ways to postpone decisive action.

Secondly, even the highly educated and philosophically inclined Prince of Denmark seems blind to aspects of his own personality that have distorted both his judgement and behaviour more generally, for example in his relationship with both his mother and with the woman whom he might have married, Ophelia—whom he drives to suicide for no fault of her own. Hamlet blames his mother for conspiring with his uncle to murder his father, when there is in fact no evidence of such a conspiracy: and he is paralyzed by his persistent anger at Queen Gertrude's incestuous behaviour in marrying his uncle so soon after the death of his father. He describes her character in universal terms:

Frailty, thy name is woman

Why is he quite so angry at his mother's infidelity? There are limits to the extent that one can probe his psychology, despite the many books written on the subject. He is, however, not the only person in a position of real or potential leadership whose behaviour has been swayed by underlying causes that are not under his full control, because he does not understand what is happening within himself.[1]

Analogies and similarities: Postponing the decision

Hamlet is thrashing around for much of the play like a fish on a hook, desperately seeking a way to avoid the destiny which he must sooner or later embrace; *and yet he is not alone.* Hamlet's behaviour is not unique. How many times is a manager or leader reluctant to make the decision that he knows, in his heart of hearts, that he must take—but which he cannot bring himself to do? Why does he seek more and more 'evidence' to convince himself of what he already knows? Why does he turn away from doing the deed himself, and look to find another means of achieving a disagreeable objective—even if that path to action be far more devious and liable to go awry, than the more obvious and straightforward option?

Consider three examples from organisational life:

1. The senior executive who puts off a decision by commissioning further research—when the relevant research has already been carried out, and the obvious but unpopular solution to the problem is already clear, not only to him, but to anyone else with a clear mind and a reasonable grasp of the relevant and easily accessible information.

2. The senior executive who brings in a 'management consultant' to fire a long-standing and loyal employee, whose only fault is that his skills are no longer needed. Since the management consultant has been paid to 'discover' what is already known, this is, in my view, hypocrisy in action and a perfect example of moral cowardice.

3. The senior executive who fails to make the right decision (by which is meant simply a well-informed, clear, objective decision, rather than the impossible option of a decision which would withstand *any* criticism) not because he lacks the relevant training or experience but because he is somehow blind about some aspect of *himself.*

His partiality or prejudice may be the result of a temporary impediment, or may have a more deep-seated cause. Whichever the case, however, it cannot be ignored, and something must be done. Some managers are more democratically inclined than others, and find it easier to communicate. Are they more likely to receive and listen to a word of advice, when it concerns themselves? Is their door really always open?

Leadership: Some issues illustrated and lessons reinforced

In the commentary to the questions that accompany each chapter, two highly influential leadership theorists are cited: John Adair on action-centred leadership, and James MacGregor Burns on transformational leadership. Both offer theories of leadership that are easily understood, and the challenge lies in their application.

That message applies more generally, for in considering this book as a whole, I realise that its lessons about leadership are simple ones and will not be new to its readers. Nor should they be. We already know, in essence, what good leadership requires. The trick is in applying in practice the lessons that we have already grasped in theory; and the literature serves to expand our understanding of how others have sought to do so and to learn from their experience.

Leadership is not impossible

The extracts have not been chosen to depress the reader about leadership and to suggest that it represents an impossible task. These fictional leaders faced very considerable challenges, and some died in addressing them. That does not mean, however, that they failed to measure up to the challenge. The failure to complete a task or achieve a goal does not necessarily indicate a failure of leadership, and nor need it engender a cynical outlook. The task may simply have proved impossible: but that cannot be known beforehand.

Leadership is a means to an end, and not an end in itself

Leadership is not a goal in itself. The purpose of leadership is to achieve an agreed outcome which would not otherwise be possible, or would be very much harder to achieve; and not to display a perfect example of leadership in abstraction.

CONCLUSION

Leadership is a shared enterprise

Who decides upon what the outcome should be? Ultimately, it is the decision of the group; for it is the group that validates the decisions of the leader. Although the timing varies, leadership is in essence a collaborative process. As Robert Jordan points out, the leader may need to act first, before he seeks the retrospective agreement of the group that what he had decided upon was the right course of action; but he will need to seek that endorsement. Leadership is not a popularity contest: but a leader who becomes *too* isolated is looking for trouble.

Captain Larsen, although the legitimate commander of the *Ghost* and a man of extraordinary confidence in his own abilities, is not a true leader, for he rules simply by force and never by persuasion, and he never seeks any kind of endorsement for his decisions.[2] There is a superficial rationality to his behaviour, in that when Van Weyden first joins his crew, it seems that Larsen is seeking to maximise the profits of the voyage. Like Captain Ahab of the *Pequod*[3], however, Larsen has his own agenda; and it will lead to disaster.

Robert Jordan is of another kind. His nationality, background and temperament distance him from the group that requires leadership, but he does not allow those potentially debilitating factors to sabotage the mission. He focuses on the task in hand, and does all he can to ensure its success. Will he succeed? The final outcome is beyond his control; but he will not fail for want of trying.

The good leader is neither world-weary cynic nor naive optimist

Some of the writers chosen, such as George Orwell or Joseph Conrad, show a pessimistic outlook on life, or at least on utopianism; but there is a difference between pessimism and cynicism. Leadership requires confidence in oneself and one's own abilities: in one's own judgement, in Jordan's enduring view; and that confidence falls somewhere between world-weary cynicism and foolish optimism.

The realistic leader accurately assesses the magnitude of the task that he faces, but does not allow this to daunt either him or those whom he is charged to inspire. He is resolute without being bombastic and he is always human. As Captain Stanhope answers, when the sergeant-major asks him what will happen *after* they have repelled the German attack:

Stanhope

Then we go on and win the war.

Sergeant-Major

Win the war. Very good, Sir.

It is pleasing to note that both men display a command of irony and share a perfect understanding. They have resolved Hamlet's dilemma; and their future is beckoning.

So is ours. An opera is judged by its performance, and not by the envy, malice and spite that may have been part of its gestation, and which are apparently part of the operatic tradition. There is a difference between rehearsal and performance, and each is necessary to the other. To read about leadership is to rehearse for one's next performance. I wish you luck with yours.

Recommended reading

We have already mentioned the sister volume to this publication:
Leadership in Literature
Edited by Jonathan Gosling and Peter Villiers
Triarchy Press, 2011
This is a lengthier text than this short volume, and examines the works of some fifteen authors from an international context.

You might also wish to consider:

Three Ways of Getting Things Done:
Hierarchy, Heterarchy and Responsible Autonomy in Organisations
Gerard Fairtlough
Triarchy Press, 2007
(International edition)
Gerard Fairtlough, the founder of Triarchy Press, explains his philosophy of leadership and management in clear and simple English, based on his own experience in scientific research and manufacture.

CONCLUSION

Finally, you may wish to read in full the texts have chosen for analysis in this book. The purpose of any work of fiction, says the playwright David Mamet (1998), is to tell a story in such a way that we continue to pay attention because we want to know what happens next; and if there is a 'message' it is for the reader or viewer to discern it. I have suggested some possible leadership issues that emerge in the chosen texts, as they have appeared to me; and you will undoubtedly discern more.

Notes

1. As the Russian psychologist L S Vygotsky (Vygotsky, 1971) points out, the explanation that Hamlet gives for finally killing his uncle at the end of the play is not the same as the motive that has dominated him for the past five acts: the urge to revenge himself upon his uncle for the death of his father. This inconsistency, real or apparent, in Hamlet's character makes him more rather than less credible as a person, and a deeper study in decision-making.
2. Is Wolf Larsen, because of his superior physical gifts, belief in himself, and confidence that he has the right solution to any problem, what was once commonly called a 'born leader'?
    I think not. Firstly, the story tells us that Larsen had an immense struggle to reach his position of command of the *Ghost*, and feels extremely bitter that he was unable to go further. Secondly, the old question as to whether leaders born or made does not deserve a simple answer. There are individuals who show a remarkable and apparently innate taste for leadership, and who may fairly be described as 'natural leaders'—although behind their apparently effortless accomplishment may lie a substantial period of preparation and rehearsal. They are often people who are described as charismatic—although there is a danger here of a circular definition, in which one unclear definition is 'explained' by another.
    However, suppose it is accepted for the sake of argument that some people find it easier to play the role of the leader than others—even if it is also granted that there is more than one way to lead, and that leadership skills can at least to a certain extent be developed by experience and practice. What, then, for those of us who were not 'born' to lead? Are we doomed to a life of subservient and unacknowledged toil—or at best the practice of an uncertain and unconvincing exercise in role play?
    Again, I think not. Firstly, we need not all be leaders, heroic or otherwise, and service is not necessarily unrewarded. Secondly, we do not remain the people we were born. We remake ourselves as we progress through life, and learn both from our experience and those of others. We may not be born a leader: but we may be reborn as one.
3. *Moby-Dick* is one of the books examined in depth in the sister volume to this publication, *Leadership in Literature*, edited by Jonathan Gosling and Peter Villiers, Triarchy Press (2011).

Bibliography

Adair, John (1973). *Action-centred leadership*. London: Kogan Page.

Bate, Jonathan (1997). *The Genius of Shakespeare*. London: Picador.

Bate, Jonathan (2008). *Soul of the Age: The Life, Mind and World of William Shakespeare*. London: Viking.

Bok, Sylvia (1978). *Lying: Moral Choice in Public and Private Life*. Sussex: Harvester Press.

Bok, Sylvia (1986). *Secrets: On the Ethics of Concealment and Revelation*. Oxford University Press.

Burns, James MacGregor (1978). *Leadership*. New York: HarperCollins.

Conrad, Joseph (2002). *Lord Jim*. Oxford University Press.

Conrad, Joseph (1984). *The Nigger of the Narcissus*. Oxford University Press.

Conrad, Joseph (2007). *The Secret Agent*. Penguin Classics.

Conrad, Joseph (1947). *The Secret Sharer 'Twixt Land and Sea*. London: J. M. Dent and Sons.

Conrad, Joseph (2002). *Under Western Eyes*. Penguin Books. Edited, with an Introduction, Notes and Appendix 'Autocracy and War', by Paul Kirschner.

Conrad, Joseph (1963). *Victory*. Penguin Modern Classics.

Crick, Bernard (1992). *George Orwell: a Life*. London: Penguin.

Gardner, Averill (1987). *George Orwell*. Boston: Twayne Publishers.

Gilmour, David (2003). *The Long Recessional: The Imperial Life of Rudyard Kipling*. London: Pimlico.

Goffman, Erving (1970). *Strategic Interaction*. Oxford: Basil Blackwell.

Gray, John (2002). *Straw Dogs*. London: Granta.

Gray, John (2004). *Heresies: Against Progress and Other illusions*. London: Granta.

Greene, Graham (1955). *The Quiet American*. London: Heinemann.

Hemingway, Ernest (2005). *For Whom The Bell Tolls*. London: Vintage Books.

Hemingway, Ernest (1957). *The Old Man and the Sea*. London: Jonathan Cape.

Howard, Sir Michael (1990). *British Intelligence in the Second World War, Volume Five: Strategic Deception*. HMSO, London.

Kipling, Rudyard (1937). *Something of Myself*. London: Macmillan.

Kipling, Rudyard (1994). *Kim*. London: Everyman.

Kipling, Rudyard (1929). *Stalky and Co.* London: Macmillan.

Kipling, Rudyard (1981). *Captains Courageous*. London: Macmillan.

London, Jack (1963). *The Bodley Head Jack London*. Edited and introduced by Arthur Calder-Marshall. London: The Bodley Head.

(Volume 1: Short Stories; The Call of the Wild; Volume 2: The Road; Volume 3: Martin Eden; Volume 4: The Klondyke Dream)

London, Jack (1904). *The Sea Wolf*. New York: Bantam Books.

Maccoby, Michael (2000). 'Narcissistic Leaders: The Incredible Pros, the Inevitable Cons', *The Harvard Business Review*, January-February, 2000.

Mamet, David (1998). *True and False: Heresy and Common Sense for the Actor*. London: Faber and Faber.

Margolick, David (2008). 'Papa's Gift to the Fire-in-the-Belly Crowd', *The New York Times*, 2 November 2008.

Marr, Andrew (2009). *The Making of Modern Britain*. Basingstoke: Macmillan.

Meyers, Jeffrey (2000). *Orwell: Wintry Conscience of a Generation*. New York: W. W. Norton & Company.

Sartre, Jean-Paul (1961). *Les Mains Sales*. London: Methuen.

Sherry, Norman (1966). *Conrad's Eastern World*. London: Cambridge University Press.

Stape, John (2007). *The Several Lives of Joseph Conrad*. London: William Heinemann.

Villiers, Peter (2006). *Joseph Conrad: Master Mariner*. Suffolk: Seafarer Books.

Villiers, Peter (2009). *Police and policing: an introduction*. Hampshire: Waterside Press.

Villiers, Peter (2010). *Gavrilo Princip: The Assassin who Started the First World War*. Devon: The Fawler Press.

Vygotsky, Lev S. (1971). *The Psychology of Art, Volume Three*. MIT Press.

Index

A

addictive personality 30
adolescence 24
adolescent 19
adolesence 14
Airstrip One 107, 111, 112
alcoholic 29, 122
allegory 5, 110
anarchist militia 101
anarchists 73, 75, 78, 79, 80, 83, 87, 89
anarchist terrorism 4
Anglo-Saxon 21
Apollo Korzeniowski 71
authority 11, 15, 56, 133

B

Barack Obama 3
barque Otago, 72
Battle of Agincourt 141
BBC 101
Belgian Congo 72
beyond good and evil 43
Big Brother 5, 107, 108, 111
blind panic 138
boarding school 15, 21
bohemianism 30
bull-fighting, 48
bureaucracy 4
Burma 97

C

Captain Hardy 124
Captain Larsen 146
Captain Stanhope 5, 121, 138, 142, 147
catharsis 107
causal chain 65
CCTV 111
censorship 109, 113
Cesare Lombroso 76

Index

Charisma 130
charismatic 106, 139
Charlotte Bronte 6
chivalry 138
Christianity 33
Christopher Plummer 138
CIA 64
civilization 22
civil war 5
Class 129
class system 129
college 29
colonialism 98
command 57
commitment 31
communism 5, 105, 110
community 22
conspiracy 71, 83
conventional morality 33, 35
corporal punishment 23
cowardic 132
crisis 122, 125
critics 29
Cuba 50, 70

D

'Death' Larsen 40
debt 29
deception 11, 75, 83, 105
decisiveness 142
democracy 109
democratic acceptance 63
democratic socialism 100, 106
destiny 143
detection 81
devious 23
Devon 11
dialogue 51
dictatorship 103, 110
discipline 22, 133
Discipline 104
discretion 84
disloyalty 22

doublethink 109
dramatic ironies 124
dramatic irony 53
drill 16
dug-out 121
dugout 5, 125
duty 5, 21, 134
dystopia 102, 109, 112

E

education 21
eloquence 16
emotional support 128
empire 9, 21
Enduring values 128
enthusiasm 31
Eric Blair 97
Erich Maria Remarque 121
Ernst Junger 121
espionage 71
Eton 97, 100, 101
evidence 143
evil 5
existentialist philosophy 70
expediency 84

F

fantasies 139
fate 53, 62
First World War 119
Flora Wellman 30

G

gender 21, 62
General Franco 64
generalship 101
George Orwell 9, 65, 69, 146
German Democratic Republic 109
Glory 16
God 59
grace under pressure 47, 54
Great War 13

Index

Greenwich Observatory 73
Greenwich Park 82

H

Hemingway 115
Henry V 141, 142
heroism 118, 139
hero-worship 129, 133, 134
hidden agenda 83, 85
Hollywood 40
homage to masculinity 53
Home Guard 101
Honour 16
hope 128
Howard Barker 138
human decency 106
human nature 59, 84, 100, 102, 128
human rights 109
humour 15

I

idealism 64, 105, 108
identity 82
'If' 9, 134
illusions 82
image and reality 6
immortality 35, 37
imperialism 9, 98
imperial rule 98
India 9, 97
individuality 11
innocence 84
intellectual 21
Intellectuals 111
intelligentsia 102, 109
interrogation 111
investigative journalism 31
irony 83, 85, 131, 147

J

Jack Gold 138
Jack London 50, 53

Jane Eyre 6, 8
Jean Paul Sartre 70
John McCain 1, 3, 66
John Stuart Mill 112
Joseph Conrad 9, 146
journalism 51
judgement of history 65
Jura 101, 109
just war 70

K

Kim 12, 23
knowledge 80, 82
Konrad Korzeniowski 71

L

Lahore 11
Laurence Olivier 127, 142
leadership 103
leadership qualities 16
learning environment 21
legitimacy 64
Lieutenant Osborne 122
Lockwood Kipling 22
Lord Jim 134
loyal 128
loyalty 3, 57, 80, 82, 84

M

man 142
manifest destiny 139
manipulation of information 83
marriage 13, 59, 84
Marseilles 71
materialism 37
maturity 134
Maud Brewster 3, 39, 40
Michael Morpurgo 139
military service 101
Military service 129
modernism 72
moral cowardice 144

Index

moral dilemmas 65, 70
morale 57

N

naïve 125
nationality 4
natural leader 17
Newspeak 107
Nietszche 33
Nietzsche 3, 43, 44
Nobel Prize 51
Nobel Prize for Literature 13
nobility 38

O

obedience 22, 65, 109
Oceania 107
Officer Training Corps 101
orders 62
originality 22
Orwell 10

P

Paris 49, 50, 100
patriotism 2, 16, 17, 108
Pavlov 111
pessimism 57, 146
Poland 71
police 79, 98, 112
Police 97
pornography 74
power 62
prejudice 31, 62
pride 61
procrastination 142
propaganda 5, 103, 104, 105
psychopath 43
public school system 129

R

race 21
racial prejudice 12

Raj 9, 13, 98
rebellion 24
rebelliousness 23
Red Ensign 72
righteousness 37
risk 56
Robert Jordan 1, 47, 146
role-play 131
Rudyard Kipling 121
Russia 71
Russian revolution 102

S

sacrifice 63, 83, 103
satire 5, 102, 104
Scapegoating 84
science fiction 31, 110
second in command 124, 128
Second Lieutenant Raleigh 122
self-esteem 132
self-knowledge 133
Senator Barack Obama 48
Senator John McCain 47
sense of humour 59
Siegfried Sassoon 133
Soviet Union 109, 110, 112
Spanish civil war 101
Spanish Civil War 47, 110
Spenser Tracy 45
Stalin 103, 106
stupidity of war 128
style 48, 51, 61
suicide 29, 50
Suicide bombers 64
superman 43, 44
Superman 33, 43
surveillance 109, 111

T

Tadeusz Bobrowski 71
telescreen 108
tension 53
Tension 127

Index

terminator 43
terrorism 112
terrorist 76, 85
The abuse of language 104
theft 19
The Secret Agent 72, 73, 79, 83, 95
Thomas Arnold 14
thought-crime 111
thought police 108
torture 108
totalitarian 109
totalitarianism 5, 104, 106, 111, 113
tradition 62
treachery 3
trenches 13
Trotksy 103
Trotsky 106
trust 55, 126
tuberculosis 102, 109
'Two Minute Hate' 107

U

utopia 5, 108
utopianism 146

V

violence 63

W

Walter Mitty 139
war poets 121
weakness 132
West End 127
William Chaney 30
Winston Churchill 120
Winston Smith 7, 107, 109
wives 49
working class 100

About the Author

Peter Villiers was born of Australian parents in Chipping Norton, Oxon, in 1947. After attending the very traditional King's School, Canterbury and the supposedly radical University of Essex (1966-1970), he then joined the army, serving in Northern Ireland, Cyprus and Hong Kong, and learning a good deal about leadership in practice. He has worked as a college principal and police adviser and is the author of many books on leadership, ethics and human rights, as well as a marine biography of Joseph Conrad and a recent study of Gavrilo Princip, the youthful and idealistic assassin whose two shots in Sarajevo led to the First World War.

About Triarchy Press

Triarchy Press is an independent publishing house that looks at how organisations work and how to make them work better. We present challenging perspectives on organisations in short and pithy, but rigorously argued, books.

For more information about Triarchy Press, or to order any of our publications, please visit our website or drop us a line:

www.triarchypress.com
info@triarchypress.com

We're now on Twitter: @TriarchyPress
and Facebook: www.facebook.com/triarchypress

Lightning Source UK Ltd.
Milton Keynes UK
175685UK00001B/50/P